OECD DOCUMENTS

IMHE
PROGRAMME
ON INSTITUTIONAL MANAGEMENT
IN HIGHER EDUCATION

Managing Information Strategies in Higher Education

PUBLISHER'S NOTE
The following texts are published in their original form to permit faster distribution at a lower cost.

ORGANISATION FOR ECONOMIC CO-OPERATION AND DEVELOPMENT

ORGANISATION FOR ECONOMIC CO-OPERATION AND DEVELOPMENT

Pursuant to Article 1 of the Convention signed in Paris on 14th December 1960, and which came into force on 30th September 1961, the Organisation for Economic Co-operation and Development (OECD) shall promote policies designed:

- to achieve the highest sustainable economic growth and employment and a rising standard of living in Member countries, while maintaining financial stability, and thus to contribute to the development of the world economy;
- to contribute to sound economic expansion in Member as well as non-member countries in the process of economic development; and
- to contribute to the expansion of world trade on a multilateral, non-discriminatory basis in accordance with international obligations.

The original Member countries of the OECD are Austria, Belgium, Canada, Denmark, France, Germany, Greece, Iceland, Ireland, Italy, Luxembourg, the Netherlands, Norway, Portugal, Spain, Sweden, Switzerland, Turkey, the United Kingdom and the United States. The following countries became Members subsequently through accession at the dates indicated hereafter: Japan (28th April 1964), Finland (28th January 1969), Australia (7th June 1971), New Zealand (29th May 1973), Mexico (18th May 1994), the Czech Republic (21st December 1995) and Hungary (7th May 1996). The Commission of the European Communities takes part in the work of the OECD (Article 13 of the OECD Convention).

The Programme on Institutional Management in Higher Education (IMHE) started in 1969 as an activity of the OECD's newly established Centre for Educational Research and Innovation (CERI). In November 1972, the OECD Council decided that the Programme would operate as an independent decentralised project and authorised the Secretary-General to administer it. Responsibility for its supervision was assigned to a Directing Group of representatives of governments and institutions participating in the Programme. Since 1972, the Council has periodically extended this arrangement; the latest renewal now expires on 31st December 1996.

The main objectives of the Programme are as follows:

- to promote, through research, training and information exchange, greater professionalism in the management of institutions of higher education; and
- to facilitate a wider dissemination of practical management methods and approaches.

*
* *

Publié en français sous le titre :
GÉRER LES STRATÉGIES DE L'INFORMATION
DANS L'ENSEIGNEMENT SUPÉRIEUR

FOREWORD

The papers presented here are the results of the OECD/IMHE project entitled "Information Management: Information Technology as an Emerging Issue for Institutional Management in Higher Education". They cover such topics as executive information systems, student-owned computing, the changing role of institutional computing centres and financial issues. Case studies complete the presentation of the issues.

The IMHE project was based on the assumption that the development of information technology (IT) in higher education is likely to have a significant impact on institutional management. Not only information technology itself, but its use and organisation will impact on higher education, based on the stage of its development and the potential achieved. Improving institutional management is the reason why it is important to influence and shape the use of IT, and to promote its potential to help achieve institutional goals and objectives.

The term "information management" not only refers to the strategic relevance of modern information technology, but also to all management issues related not only to technology itself, but to the strategic use and handling of information, to strategic information systems, and to the resources infrastructure needed in order to implement information strategies.

TABLE OF CONTENTS

Chapter 1

GENERAL INTRODUCTION

Chapter 2

FROM COMPUTING STRATEGY TO INFORMATION STRATEGY
by Edgar Frackmann

Chapter 3

FINANCING, BUDGETING, AND CHARGING PROBLEMS RELATED TO INFORMATION TECHNOLOGY IN HIGHER EDUCATION
by Edgar Frackmann

Chapter 4

STUDENT-OWNED COMPUTING
by Gordon Bull

Chapter 5

EXECUTIVE INFORMATION SYSTEMS FOR INSTITUTIONAL MANAGEMENT IN HIGHER EDUCATION
by Edgar Frackmann

Chapter 6

THE CHANGING ROLE OF INSTITUTIONAL COMPUTING CENTRES
by Edgar Frackmann

Chapter 7

IMPLEMENTING AN INFORMATION STRATEGY
The case of the Vienna University of Economics and Business Administration
by Barbara Sporn and George Miksch

Chapter 8

THE MANAGEMENT OF A CAMPUS NETWORK
The case of the University of Hong Kong
by John Dockerill

Chapter 9

INFORMATION STRATEGIES
A UK perspective
by Peter Ford

Chapter 1

GENERAL INTRODUCTION

by

Edgar Frackmann

Hochschul-Informations-Systems (HIS) GmbH, Hannover (Germany)

The papers presented here are based on and are the result of the OECD/IMHE project entitled "Information Management: Information Technology as an Emerging Issue for Institutional Management in Higher Education". The IMHE project was launched based on the assumption that the development of information technology (IT) in general, and its ubiquity in higher education, are likely to have significant impacts on institutional management in higher education. Not information technology itself, but its use and organisation will impact higher education, based on the stage of its development and the potential it achieved. Improving institutional management is the reason why it is important to influence and shape the use of IT, and to promote the benefits of its potential for the achievement of institutional goals and objectives.

While defining the scope and domain of its research field, the project began with the term "information management". The project thus referred to observations made in the business world, having in mind the idea that major trends in business are not totally unrelated to what happens or should happen in higher education. "Information management" is a term used in the corporate world in order to emphasise a new role of information and information technology for the survival and competitive advantage of companies in their environment of competitors, clients, and suppliers. Dealing with information technology as hardware and software (*i.e.* technological infrastructure and information systems) it is important to keep in mind that the use and the handling of information is the primary purpose of information technology development and application. The use of information, its processing, dissemination, and transmission (and thus the implementation of information technology) has gained a strategic dimension in industry, *e.g.* it is linked more closely to the overall company strategy. However, whether the same is true for higher education is the question, acknowledging that higher education is an "information intensive industry": handling and transfer of information is the primary purpose of higher education and research.

The term "information management" does not only refer to the strategic relevance of modern information technology, but also to all management issues related not only to technology, but to strategic use and handling of information, to strategic information systems, and to information resources infrastructure, needed in order to implement information related strategies. The conceptualisation of information management for the IMHE project, as well as for the contributions presented here, is comprised of a three-layered structure of management issues as depicted in Figure 1.1.

Information handling may be relevant in two circumstances in higher education:

– in the course of the primary processes, *i.e.* teaching and learning on the one hand, and research on the other, these primary processes rely on supporting functions with regard to information provision and information access: libraries and information services; and

– in the context of institutional management and administration, and in the context of public relations, marketing, attracting clients, organising the production processes, evaluating the outcomes and the quality of higher education services, fulfilling the accountability and reporting requirements of the governments and the interested public (Figure 1.2).

For a project focusing on general management issues of information handling and information technology in higher education, it is essential to identify the general characteristics of management issues in all the main areas identified. For the primary processes, at first glance, general management concerns related to the transfer and handling of information in teaching, learning and research seem to be limited. Teaching, learning, and research are highly decentralised processes, and further decentralisation of IT-related issues is nurtured by tendencies to downsize IT resources. With regard to information management and information technology issues in the primary processes, general management is however involved to the extent that more centralised provision of resources and services are needed. In this context, general management issues might include matters of financing, budgeting, organisational structure, personnel policies, technological infrastructure (*e.g.* networking infrastructure), organisational culture issues, government/higher education relationships and inter-institutional co-operation and competition.

For the second domain -- information and information technology for management and administration, and for organisational survival -- these issues are at the core of information management as concern of general institutional management in higher education. While the IMHE project goal focuses on general management issues linked to information technology, it is evident that such a project must begin with a thorough review of the role of information technology and the information technology platform in higher education. However, it is not issues such as network management or management of a computing centre or library information technology, but general management issues in a networked organisation, and general management issues related to the role of central information and information technology services, which are of concern to the project and its audience. The aim of the first phase of the project is to :

– investigate the state-of-the-art of information technology in European higher education;

– identify the potential of information technology for higher education; and

– identify the general management issues related to information technology for institutional decision-makers and decision-making structures.

In this first phase, and for the purpose of the investigation's aims, five country/ institution case studies have been undertaken by the five project members, focusing on their respective countries of origin (France, Germany, Ireland, the Netherlands, and United Kingdom). The general issues were discussed intensively among group members and documented in the Jessica Kingsley publication: *Information Technology: Issues for Higher Education Management* (Higher Education Policy Series 26, Jessica Kingsley, London). It is important here to thank the authors of this publication and project members for their valuable contribution which indeed helped to set the foundations for further investigations in the project and beyond.

In reference to the three-layered structure of information management, the starting point for the investigation was the identification of information systems (applications) in higher education, followed by investigation in more detail, particularly their stage of development and their actual and future potential for higher education (Figure 1.3).

The five application areas of information technology identified in this first phase and investigated in more detail, were:

- teaching and learning;

- research;

- administration;

- management; and

- libraries and information services.

Apart from these investigations, the identification of special management issues, which are the focus of a second phase of the project, was reinforced by discussions and feed-back material provided by the participants of a seminar in Paris in December 1991. All the participants of this seminar played a pivotal role in the successful and fruitful continuation of the project.

The four topics, *i.e.* special management issues, which were deemed appropriate and worthy of further detailed elaboration were:

- executive information systems for higher education management;

- student-owned computing and the electronic campus;

- the changing role of institutional computing centres; and

- financing, budgeting, charging related to information technology.

Two of these topics refer to the application level of the three-layered information management structure (EIS and educational applications), where the EIS topic is very close to the managerial use of information issue (*i.e.* the information layer). The other two topics refer, not to the technological infrastructure, but to the organisational and financial infrastructure for the use of information and information systems (Figure 1.4).

The idea of this phase was to apply a so-called workshop concept in order to approach these four topics in more detail. Some ten to fifteen experts in their respective fields were called on for each topic, in order to assemble for a two-day expert workshop. The workshops consist of very intensive discussions between small groups of experts, and a so-called management briefing, produced based on participant input. The experts who participated in the workshops, making available their time, efforts and expertise in the field, were crucial for the success of this phase of the project.

Workshop	Date	Location	Participants
Student-owned Computing and the Electronic Campus	September 1992	Brighton, UK	Christer Alvegård Dick Jan Bierman Gordon Bull Edgar Frackmann Hans Köhler Bruno Lemaire Lawrence M. Levine T. Alex Reid John Stephenson Javier Torrealdea Clive Walters
Executive Informations Systems for Higher Education Management	October 1992	Kassel, Germany	Lore Alkier M.P. Angenent Hans Brinkmann Edgar Frackmann John Fürstenberg Josef M. Häussling Peter Lykke Helmut A.O. Krcmar Leo Mannhart W.R. McDonough Bernhard Nagel Christoph Oehler Reinhard Pfab Kyösti Pulliainen Thomas A.H. Schöck Frits Schutte Gerhard Selmayr Neil Spoonley Conrad Steinemann Paul LeVasseur
The Changing Role of Institutional Computing Centres	June 1993	Loccum, Germany	Jean Louis Delahaye Yves Epelboin H. Felsch Edgar Frackmann David F. Hartley Dennis Jennings Karl-Wilhelm Neubauer Bruno Paternostre Ole Carsten Pedersen H. Pralle Allan Robiette Kristel Sarlin
Financing, Budgeting, Charging related to Information Technology	February 1994	Sils-Maria, Switzerland	Hans-Peter Axmann Edgar Frackmann Rolf Gengenbach Jürgen Harms Karl Kurbel Bruno Lix Dieter Maass Arne Moi Frits Schutte Mike Tedd

For the third and concluding phase of this project, the idea was to approach general management issues related to information processing, information systems and information technology in a more comprehensive, integrated and unifying way. A couple of case studies, *i.e.* intensive discussions with relevant individuals at higher education institutions in five European countries, helped identify "Institutional Information Strategy" as the all integrating topic for institutional management[1]. A final seminar of the IMHE project in Paris in 1995 provided three cases which may be regarded as an additional background for the general papers. These cases are presented by the institutional members involved.

Information technology and information systems may be used in higher education in a strategic way -- they may contribute significantly to the strategic use and handling of information in order to achieve the strategic goals and objectives of a higher education institution. This is the underlying assumption of **Chapter 2** entitled "From computing strategy to information strategy". This chapter urges general institutional management to take the initiative to develop an institutional information strategy. While former strategies in this context focused mainly on technology, today these strategies must emphasize information use and handling, and refer to the strategic issues in this context and to the overall institutional strategy. They must deal with three challenges the higher education institutions are facing: *the informational challenge*, leading to more demanding information processing in the primary (teaching and research) as well as in the managerial processes; *the technological challenges*, information technology bearing the potential in itself to revolutionise higher education as an information-intensive business; and finally *the policy and financing challenge*, related to IT issues, referring to major changes in this domain of higher education policy and financing. The chapter provides a checklist for an institutional information strategy.

Whatever activity and whatever policy, funds are needed, resources must be deployed and allocated, and financial decisions need to be made. Dealing with financial issues, however, does not mean posing questions about where the money should come from, and how it should be passed on to those who need it. It also means dealing with information policy, the role of information technology in this context, the changing environment and characteristics of information technology, as well as setting priorities of efficiency, effectiveness and institutional culture. The financing topics focus most comprehensively on the core issues for institutional management in higher education with regards to information technology, information systems and information handling. **Chapter 3**, "Financing, budgeting, and charging problems related to information technology in higher education", provides a comprehensive view of financing issues, recommendations and a list of IT-related indicators for higher education.

Chapter 4, "Student-owned computing", does more than simply deal with policies of institutions requiring students to own computers. This was the initial idea, in 1991 when IMHE seminar participants asked the project group to continue investigating details of IT-related management issues. However, it turned out that, with or without such a policy, an increasing number of students have access to computers. From an institutional policy, it suddenly became important for everyone to be on the network, and is becoming increasingly so. A machine and network-saturated campus is the

---

[1] I would like to thank all the interviewees at the Vienna Economics University in Austria, Umea University in Sweden, University of Joensuu and the Technical University of Helsinki in Finland, Heriot Watts University, University of Edinburgh, University of Nottingham, London School of Economics in United Kingdom and at all the German Universities for their patience and time devotion.

result of an unrelenting appetite for services in the network. The "Electronic Campus" is emerging, with intended and unintended effects on educational goals and tasks of institutions -- challenging teachers and managers equally (Figure 1.5).

This chapter treats the overall topic of educational applications, which are based on students having computers and access to a campus network. The educational applications are related to the educational and institutional goals and objectives, as well as to the infrastructure required in order to use these educational applications (Figure 1.6).

An Executive Information System (EIS) is the front-end of computerised information services for institutional managers. An EIS supports the systematic use and processing of information in the course of managerial processes, but it also provides the managers with access to the more informal information and communication channels within and outside the institution where increasingly electronic media are used. **Chapter 5**, "Executive Information Systems for institutional management in higher education", provides institutional managers with one of the most important issues, while dealing with information technology, information systems and use of information: it is the issue of their own IT support. The chapter helps understand the general issues of EIS, as well as the role of an EIS in a "flat" organisation such as higher education.

The development of information and communication technology poses important questions for institutional managers, with regard to the information-resources related services within a higher education institution. **Chapter 6**, "The changing role of institutional computing centres", uses the formerly so-called computing centres as the most important example (apart from the central library), to deal with questions of central or decentral provisions of services, outsourcing, top slicing or charging, merging of information and information resources related services, creating the service orientation. General managers as the clientele of this whole volume should become familiar with the internal problems and service-related problems of the computing centres when they decide about financing and organisational issues within their institutions.

The three case studies presented after the more general chapters emphasize different aspects, but all deal with issues of information strategies:

- **Chapter 7**, "Implementing an information strategy. The case of the Vienna University of Economics and Business Administration" provides an example of a successful strategy of implementing a new use of information technology. It is very interesting to learn about implementation strategies including internal marketing, promotion and PR.

- **Chapter 8**, "The management of a campus network. The case of the University of Hong Kong" provides an example of a systematic planning from scratch within a young university, where technology can be implemented not only following the institutional strategies but also the latest state-of-the-art from the technological viewpoint.

- **Chapter 9**, "Information strategies. The case of UK universities", deals with the recommendations the British Joint Information Systems Committee (JISC) of the universities is developing for the use by the institutions.

Figure 1.1. **Conceptualisation of information management**

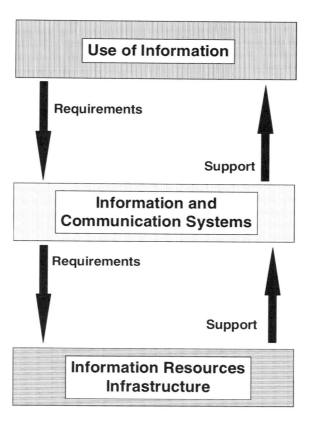

Figure 1.2. **Information handling in higher education and general management issues**

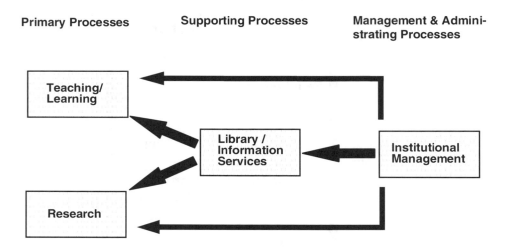

Figure 1.3. **Information systems in higher education
-- the starting point for the IMHE project**

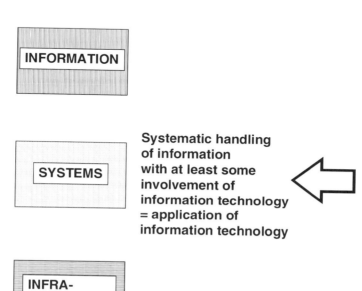

Figure 1.4. **General management issues (workshop topics)**

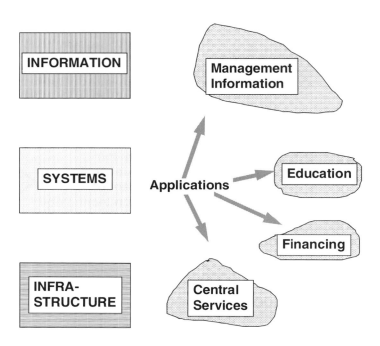

Figure 1.5. **Student-owned computing**

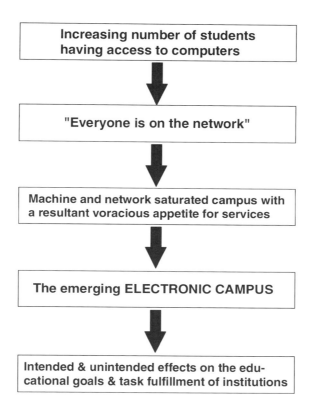

Figure 1.6. **Student-owned computing**

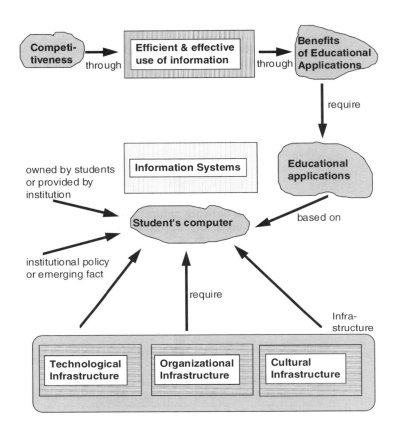

Chapter 2

FROM COMPUTING STRATEGY TO INFORMATION STRATEGY

by

Edgar Frackmann

Introduction

The development and use of information technology in higher education gave rise to the question as to whether general institutional management should deal with questions of information technology, and as to whether information technology is an issue for rectors, presidents, deans and department heads, as well as for secretary generals and the administrative department heads.

The answer to this question is definitively: No. General institutional managers should not fear that they now must share their scarce time with the "hackers" and others who enjoy switching on and off the technological details of their tiny computers, or racing on the international network, or penetrating into the ever new niches of technology and computerised information bits. General managers do not have to become *acquainted* with information technology, but they must *tackle* the potential of information technology.

In what way can information technology have a potential for higher education? Information technology is not an aim in itself. It plays a service role, perhaps even play the most crucial role in serving the handling, processing, transferring, storing of and access to information. The issue, in reality, is *information* more than information technology, and the main issue for general management in higher education is not information technology management, but *information management*.

For further elaboration it is important to keep in mind the three-layer concept which links information with information technology by requirements and support relationships. While using and handling information, there may be certain requirements concerning information systems that support the use and handling of information. And the information systems might themselves rely on the support of an information resources infrastructure, including information technology (Figure 2.1).

In order to be more precise, and to systematically approach the requirements-support (or purpose and means) chain, the institutional goals and objectives which might include competitive advantage must first be outlined. Institutions of higher education might wish, or see the need, to use information efficiently and effectively in order to achieve the institutional goals and objectives in their teaching and research tasks, maybe more efficiently and effectively than their competitors. In using or handling information efficiently and effectively, they rely on "applications" of an information resources infrastructure. "Applications" means the systematic handling of information with at least some involvement of information technology. But it is not technology (*i.e.* hardware, software, networks) which is considered the "information resources infrastructure", it is equally the organisation (*i.e.* staff and services structure, co-ordination mechanisms and decision-making structures implemented, and finance structures), and culture of the organisation under review (the basic assumptions and behaviour of those involved, concerning the use of information and information technology) which makes up the information resources infrastructure, and which might be more or less suitable to serve the efficient and effective use of information.

Why is it so important for general management in higher education to deal with these issues of information management, *e.g.* the relationship between information, information systems and information resources infrastructure? Why did it become increasingly important to deal with information management issues in today's higher education?

The main purpose of higher education (be it in its teaching or its research functions) is to deal with information. If there are major alterations in information technology, they might well be of some importance for such an information intensive enterprise as higher education. A higher education institution might gain competitive advantages while benefiting from the use of information technology and the information resources infrastructure.

There is a tendency all over Europe for higher education institutions to be granted more institutional autonomy from their governments, but they are at the same time held more accountable for the outcome and quality of their services. In this context institutional management must deal more with management, evaluation, and accountability-related information.

Information technology has already penetrated higher education. Whether institutions like it or not, students come with their own computers and expect related services, be it in teaching functions or in extracurricular activities. Information technology absorbs quite a proportion of the institutional budget and thus cannot just be an issue of managerial attention. It plays an eminent role in institutional priority decisions regarding the spending of funds available.

There is much talk about the information society, and the increasing role of information handling and information technology in social and economic life, including the competitiveness of the European economy. Higher education and research play an eminent role in this area, considering the fact that higher education institutions are the place where research for the future and education for the future is expected to be underway.

Finally, as another issue which makes information management so important for general higher education management are some dramatic changes regarding information technology and the financing of information technology, which altogether affect organisational and financial issues on the institutional level and beyond.

Dealing with information in higher education

Dealing with information first before approaching the questions of information technology means identifying where information is handled in higher education. Only a comprehensive view of information handling might help to identify the converging and synergetic aspects of information technology and help to benefit most from the potential of information technology (Figure 2.2).

Higher education is to be seen as a service provider, for which purpose it receives funds (in exchange) from students, their parents, industries, and most importantly from governments, representing the society as a whole. It is important here to identify the flow of information inherent in these exchange processes. There are *ex ante*, *ex post* and accompanying information flows, such as marketing, contracting (*ex ante*) and evaluation, accountability, reporting (*ex post*), and monitoring. What is most important with higher education is the fact that information is not only an additional element of exchange between service provider and service receiver, information is the main ingredient of the service provision processes themselves. Thus, the primary processes as well as the administrative and managerial processes in higher education deal with information. Not only the exchange processes between the institution as a whole and its environment may be conceived as processes where information plays the dominant role, but also within higher education institutions there exist exchange processes in the context of the managerial, supporting and primary processes (Figure 2.3).

To sum up the information processing in higher education, three processes relevant in this context can be identified:

1. Primary processes

   – information processing in the context of teaching and learning;
   – information processing in the context of research.

2. Supporting processes

   – information processing in the context of library and information access (library and information services);
   – communication processes and network services.

3. Managerial and administrative processes

   – evaluation;
   – decision-making;
   – contracting, accountability, reporting;
   – public relations;
   – marketing;
   – central and decentralised administration and their interrelations.

Why is it increasingly important to view, manage, and plan the information resources infrastructure that serves the information processing in higher education, only together and comprehensively?

The information services relying on the information resources infrastructure are "converging". They all tend to have the same physical common access, *i.e.* users will have the same "terminal" to whatever information processing with which they are involved and wish to participate: managerial, administrative, information retrieval, or learning and research-related communication. Also for the physical carriers, the network is in common for all the information processes mentioned. And the more one views the basic production processes in higher education, the less clear is the distinction between the primary, supporting and managerial processes. The management information, administrative information, and delivery of information is very closely related to an individual course, as compared with their relationship on more general institutional levels. Finally, it is the technology which does not further allow to conceive and plan the information and communication processes separately: computing and communication facilities are heavily intertwined and cannot further be handled the one without the other, having in view the services which are expected from technology.

Impacts of information technology

Information technology is the vehicle to deal with information, and information contents. Without any doubt, information technology has been developed to provide facilities which lead to the proclamation of an information technology revolution, as well as to the assumption that it is information technology which makes the difference or is even the cause of a different revolutionary handling of information. Thus, the question is raised whether it is the "vehicle" that changes the "contents", or whether in this present stage of information technology use, it is not necessary to focus on the technology but rather on the contents, *i.e.* the information to be handled. Contradictory statements therefore arise: one which stresses the "post"-technology stage, emphasizing the contents:

> "We have passed the stage when the vehicle for the information was of primary importance and now need to look at the potential of the systems for disseminating information and the issues concerning content, ownership, control and management of information that this throws up." (from the University of Edinburgh Informations Systems Strategy).

and the other statements which see information technology as the primary source of alterations.

> "The revolution is the difference that technology makes in how we organise, structure, and empower our lives and our workplaces." (from CAUSE).

In this context the information society is regarded as the society that is "enabled" by the advances of information technology.

It might be regarded as a question of the "chicken or the egg". Without any doubt, information technology would not have been developed into the stage which it achieved today, if there were not a desire and a need to handle information in a more efficient, effective, comprehensive, delightful and revolutionary way. And once the "vehicle" is developed, it provides a certain pressure on each individual or institution, who do not yet use it according to its potential. It is thus the potential, the enabling forces of information technology that seem to have the impact on the (information) society as a whole and on higher education specifically.

The arguments concerning the impact of information technology reflect both the scepticism and the euphoria with regard to the potential of information technology. They also reflect that information technology has contradictory impacts, which means that the impact of information technology is still dependent on whether and how information technology is used in organisations and in individual life. Consider some of these arguments, which might sound quite familiar:

(1) *The use of information technology leads to isolation of the individual. Universities do not just deliver information, they have to provide an environment for learning. Education, learning needs interaction, and it takes place in a mix of formal and informal settings. The use of information technology for the learning processes means isolation of the individual information receiver.*

Having followed the "isolation impact arguments" so far, it seems to be very easy to contribute just the contrary arguments with regard to IT impacts: Information technology enables and enhances integration. Never before was it possible for students to interact so much in a formal and informal way with their teachers and tutors as well as with their classmates. The climate of teaching and learning is changing. The codified form of learning has stepped back to a certain extent. There is great freedom of time and space. Teachers and students may talk to each other prior to their meeting, and when they meet in the classroom they are all better prepared . Information technology may not only contribute to a flattening of the organisation regarding the teacher-student relationship, but also within the formal organisation. Decisions may be decentralised, because information may be made available at the centre as well as at the basis at the same time. Thus, IT may contribute to both the decentralisation of the organisation as well as the integration of the organisation, based on the same information available and accessible everywhere in the organisation.

(2) *The individual teacher, the department heads and deans, the rectors and secretary general of the institutions do not want the information provided them through information technology. They do not really appreciate the value added by information technology, with regard to information supply.*

Indeed, information technology may contribute to an information overload, and many managers already suffer an information overload. But, the more autonomy and responsibility an organisational unit (the university, the faculty, or the department) has for the services to be delivered in exchange for the funds received, the more their managers might have to rely on information, *i.e.* information on the "markets" for their services, information on the quality and quantity of their output, and information on their clients and on the image/reputation of their organisation. Willingly or not, managers have to use information to become successful managers of successful organisations. Features of information technology may not only contribute to let the information more easily reach the managers and the individuals of the professional organisation, but it may also help select the relevant information. Thus, IT may contribute to both information pollution and the value added through information supply.

(3) *There is still resistance to use computerised information and communication facilities. It is the keyboard (typing) which is not a usual information handling device for many information users. And eventually response time, system and network interrupts and breaks, dependence on service people, etc. nourish the reluctance of many expected users.*

However, information technology is moving closer and closer to the traditional information users' habits and conveniences. Also, standards are developing that facilitate the usage once it has been learnt. But, there will always be some obstacles to be overcome, including the obstacle to be prepared to use information in a more or less systematic way. It is similar to using public telephones in so many countries and cities as long as the individual is not endowed with the total international mobility of mobile phones, or the public transportation systems which rely on their users' acquaintance with the thousands of ticket machines that exist throughout the world. Thus, access to computerised information and communication facilities requires some information and information technology related culture within an institution.

(4) *The centres loose their importance.*

The computing centre, the central library, the central lecture halls -- their physical, space-related existence is vanishing increasingly, their locality has a decreasing relevance. Access to these centres and their service personnel has been buffered so far by the need to access them physically. With information and communication technology, they may be accessed directly. Service agents from the back room, *i.e.* the reference librarians, and the information access facilitators, come to the electronic front desks. From a buffered service, it is a move to a real time service. An increasing service orientation of the "centres" may come to bear. And, computerised self-service systems, if necessarily tutored by service agents, may be implemented increasingly. Access to bibliographical information and even to publications is being broadened and liberated from its former locality. In short, the centres lose their importance as centres, but not as service units, with services offered which are related to information and information technology.

(5) *Information technology produces a chaos of costing.*

The top-sliced lump sum financing of the network facilities in higher education and research world-wide lead to the spread and success of Internet. Now, it is not only the communication that is facilitated, but also the access to information, to software, and to publications. There are enthusiasts providing information in the network who do not only contribute to an information overload, but also threaten the cost of information. Learning material offered in an open network by one university may benefit others who did not pay for it. And, the university members benefit (without being charged) from others who entered, *e.g.* bibliographical information, teaching material, or news in publicly available files. What are the costs of information, of instruction in a networked information society's higher education system? Where are they to be budgeted? Should institutions move deliberately to distance-learning? What does this mean for a potentially changing student population, a departure from the traditional students? Length of studies will no more play a role as an indicator of institutions' performance -- students may live where the living costs are moderate. What about the formal structure, the recognition of such an open international system of the "invisible college"?

(6) *The kind of information supply may change dramatically.*

It is first necessary to define what it meant by "publication". Some pieces of information were made public after a process of preparation, completion and adjustment to the final format of presentation. Now, publishing may mean moving towards a gradual completion in a process of more or less public interaction. Thus, there is more than just a shift from the paper to the electronic form of multiplication and printing on demand. But, still the process of publication in this new sense has to be structured, for example, the problems of property rights.

What is learned from these arguments concerning so-called impacts of information technology that have been gathered in this context so far? Information technology has no impacts per se. Only with a specific use of the most advanced features of information technology, is it possible to change the way of handling information. The arguments reflect contradictory tendencies that are assigned to the impact of information technology. This seems to provide the evidence again that information technology does not lead to any impact by itself. It depends on what is made of IT, how and for what purpose IT is used in organisations and for the delivery of services. The existence of a certain stage of information technology, which has the potential to revolutionise the way information is handled, forces higher education institutions to react. In such a stage, and with such a potential of IT, it has to be dealt with from the top of the institutions and its subunits, comprehensively, and as a strategic matter. Higher education institutions need an information strategy.

The foundations for an information strategy

The previous section concludes that there is an interdependence between the need for information handling in higher education institutions and information technology (Figure 2.4).

In higher education institutions, information is being handled in the above-mentioned managerial, administrative, supportive, educational, and research context. Information processing is supported by information technology. There are challenges higher education is facing with regard to information handling. Financial stringency, and more demanding clients, force institutions to provide their instructional services in a more efficient and effective way. Institutional management has to deal with information, due to an increasing institutional autonomy and more demanding accountability requirements from governments and the public. These challenges lead to more demanding information handling in higher education settings.

Information and communication technology are moving to a more advanced stage of broadened facilities and conveniences, speed and access, performance, user friendliness and reliability. This move is based on research and development, to which higher education institutions contribute considerably. It is this advanced stage of information technology which may not only serve the more demanding information handling requirements, but which may even revolutionise the way information is handled and organised in higher education, as exemplified in the previous section.

Altogether, two forces may be identified which have their impact on the "more demanding information handling" and which make higher education institutions develop an information strategy. There are the challenges higher education institutions are facing with regard to their financial, political and "market" environment on the one hand ("informational challenges"), and the challenges coming from the advanced stage of information and communication technology. A third force, which has not been depicted above, has to be taken into account, while developing an information strategy, and might be called the IT policy and financing challenges, which have their source in changes of governmental decision-making and financing modes in the IT domain.

A strategy always starts with an analysis of Strengths and Weaknesses and Opportunities and Threats, or a SWOTS analysis. While the strengths and weaknesses refer to the inner-institutional potentials and assets or lack of such, the opportunities and threats refer to the institutional environment (Figure 2.5).

In order to analyse the strengths and weaknesses, one may rely on the three layers of information management and identify the applications, the information technology infrastructure, the organisational infrastructure and the human capital and cultural infrastructure as the main assets or developmental areas upon which the information strategy may rely (Figure 2.6).

In order to analyse the opportunities and threats deriving from the environment, it is important to focus on the three challenges identified above: the informational challenges, the technological challenges, and the IT policy and financing challenges (Figure 2.7).

The remainder of this section will be devoted to identifying the challenges higher education is facing from its environment. While the strengths and weakness are institution specific, the external opportunities and threats show some common trait for all institutions in a given time period.

Information challenges

Institutions are increasingly granted more autonomy from governments. This implies that the decisions are to be made by the institutions instead of governments, be it on the all-institution level or the faculty and departmental level. For these decisions -- what programmes to be offered, production function (funds to be used), the curriculum and course structure and examinations, regulations, personnel, recruitment and salary decisions, organisational structure decisions, how many students and which students to attract and enrol, tuition fees related decisions -- information is definitely needed. At the same time, governments and the public expect more information about the performance and quality of the institutions' output (accountability information, reporting).

Higher education institutions and their subunits are regarded as service organisations. They are expected to provide educational and research services and are increasingly exposed to a market-like situation, *e.g.* financing mechanisms according to demand, or according to output. Also, service links are being established within institutions. In some countries and institutions, departments must rent the lecture halls and office rooms they needed for their undergraduate or graduate teaching, and they must pay the rent out of their institutional budgets. All these phenomena mean that informal decision-making no longer suffices, and decisions must be based on information.

In a decentralised, flat organisation, such as higher education institutions, the more service orientation and autonomy implemented, the more information may serve as the organisational glue as a whole. The same information everywhere may contribute to coherent decentralised decision-making and to common understandings and views. Shared information may be the basis for shared values and perceptions of an organisation as a whole.

Institutions may achieve competitive advantage if they provide their members (*i.e.* staff and students) with access to information in the international network; they may gain competitive advantage by using and offering innovative information technology-based teaching methods and facilities; and they may realise productivity gains in the teaching function while relying on information technology.

Be it in the teaching, research, or management domain of information handling, higher education has to cope with the explosion of information. A new IT-literate (cyberfit) generation is entering higher education, and it is no longer a question as to whether an institution should ask its students to own a computer, but whether it provides the students having a computer with access to the network facilities which allow them to use their computers for their learning and working advancements.

Technological challenges

What are the main, already existing, or future traits of an information and communication technology that challenges an information-intensive organisation, such as the university?

There are four characteristics of advanced information technology that should be mentioned while talking about the potential of IT for higher education:

- the high-speed information highways with merging technologies and converging channels for transferring information in whatever form;

- user-friendly, flexible, mobile, intelligent access tools with end-user conformed retrieval, filtering, selection, conversion, and interpretation facilities;

- the accessibility of information wherever it is needed; and

- the digital integration of information in whatever form and media it exists and may be needed (multimedia-integration).

This, of course, is the "maximum" characterisation of information technology as it may be imagined today. It does not, however, reflect the stage of technologically and economically feasible technology available and reliable. But, what happens when information technology and its economic feasibility move faster than any technological development in history?

IT policy and financing challenges

These challenges have their origin in the widespread implementation and use of information technology, its maturity and changing patterns of procurement and financing of information technology. Institutions nowadays rely heavily on the IT infrastructure. IT is indispensable for the fulfilment of the tasks of a higher education institution. One has to take into account that IT, as other investments, has investment cycles with new investment funds needed. IT today consists of smaller units (in terms of price and space) than used to be the case in the central computer mainframe phase. As a consequence, there is not a cyclical huge amount of money necessary, but a steady flow of money to keep the wide-spread smaller units up-to-date. And, it is not only reinvestment due to age and usage, but investment due to technical obsolescence, which is necessary, regarding the speed at which development and renewal take place in the field of IT.

A contradiction needs to be addressed: the majority of procurement decisions is made decentralised, due to the "smallness" of the investment units. But one important component of the IT infrastructure is the network. In spite of the independence of decentralised decision-makers, this means an even greater dependence on consensus, co-ordination, and central investments and services than in the mainframe age, as the network is not only the internal infrastructure, but also provides the crucial links to the external communication and services for the institution, and its members.

Many components of IT have become mature, they are widely used, and they are no longer an unquestioned focus of innovative investments. The question of charging for the use of IT infrastructure is raised in contrast to the encouragement for innovative use through free-of-charge access. There is a clear expectation that IT has to show efficiency and productivity gains with regard to the information handling it serves, and information processing itself (information gathering, generating, storage, dissemination) has to be cost-effective equally. Expenditures for IT are scrutinised with regard to their efficiency contribution more than before. Governments and fund allocating buffer bodies depart from top-sliced earmarked IT budgets, to give the institutions (and the institutions to give the subunits) the full discretion to determine priorities with regard to IT investments.

All these facts form a changing IT policy and financing environment, and they pose new questions, problems and decision-making situations for the institutions and their subunits, which have to be taken into account, while developing an institutional information strategy.

What is an institutional information strategy?

Before dealing with the details of an information strategy, one should be clear about what an information strategy is, and what it is not. It seems to be interesting to devote some considerations to what the history of strategies reveals.

Indeed, it is not the first time that strategies are being developed that have something to do with information technology and information management. Looking back into history, one can first identify so-called *Computing Strategies*. They refer to the plans concerning investments in the central computing power, which used to be the only or the main IT facility of higher education institutions in the era of the mainframes. In essence, it dealt with the strategies concerning the institutional computing centres, their services, their investment and reinvestment plans.

The next step in history of strategies related to information management and information technology shows a first renaming of the strategies under review. The *IT Strategies* still have their main focus on the technology, but not only are central computers making up the infrastructure, but networks are increasingly playing the role of the main infrastructural components.

A departure from the mere technical emphasis of the strategies came into view and consideration with another renaming: it is not the technology which must be planned at first hand, but the applications which should be supported by the technology. Thus, the new strategic plans deserve the denomination of *Information Systems Strategies*. Today, institutions are prepared to increasingly develop the *Information Strategy*. It is the use and handling of information which should guide the considerations and plans with regard to systems and infrastructure (Figure 2.8).

After this historical review, one may more easily define what an institutional information strategy is. An information strategy is the plan for institutional information management, which starts with the information policy of an institution, and incorporates plans for the applications of information systems and the infrastructure required for implementing the policy and the information systems. Infrastructure includes technical, organisational, and cultural components and facets. An institutional information strategy might be conceived as embedded in a system of concentric circles. The information strategy relies on and is part of an institutional strategy, thus it is only the second (embedded) circle in such a conceptualisation. But, it embraces information systems and the infrastructure strategy, which themselves are embedded in the information strategy (Figure 2.9).

The traditional concepts of strategies, mainly from the era of information systems strategies, usually have three main parts, focusing on:

- *Management Information Systems* (MIS) -- this part includes the plans for administrative and management computing;

- *Academic Applications* -- the majority of the considerations in this part are usually devoted to the library, as other academic computing facilities and applications are decided decentrally and do not fall under the grasp of the central planning efforts; and

– *Network* -- this part usually includes all the services that fall into the realm of the now changed computing centre (information resources centre).

These traditional strategies have some shortcomings with regard to what an information strategy for today's institutional information management should be.

They are too closely linked to organisational units, as they might exist traditionally within the institutions: MIS -- department, library and computing centre (or whatever its name and function may be today). Thus, these plans reflect more the functional manager's view than the general management view of information management and strategic issues of information handling, information systems and infrastructure. They are still too technology-focused and technology-centred, in contrast to an information orientation, and information as the starting-point of strategic thinking. In the same vein falls the missing link to the institutional strategy. The three-sectional structures of the strategic plans also seem to under-emphasize some informational functions which deserve central attention: public relations, marketing, and computer-aided learning do not fit very well into the structure mentioned. Altogether, such a structure tends to give little room for the cross-functional and synergetic perspectives to which modern information technology might open, for which, however, the strategy has to be approached more comprehensively and from the information perspective, instead of from the organisational or technological perspective.

A checklist for an information strategy

The aim of the following section is to provide a checklist for an institutional information strategy which takes into account the considerations developed here. At the beginning, this paper identified a three-layered concept of what is to be considered when focusing on information management. It identified information handling as the upper layer of this conceptual system, relying on the support of information systems and defining requirements concerning these information systems. And, it identified information systems as the middle layer, the application layer with regard to infrastructure. Finally, it identified the infrastructure layer, the support layer for the two upper layers, consisting itself of technological, organisational and cultural infrastructure. This three-layered concept of a support/requirements relationship should also guide an information strategy and build its core structure (Figure 2.10).

The strategy thus might have three sections:

– visions, goals, and objectives of an information-based university;

– visions, goals and objectives with regard to applications; and

– implementation strategies: technological, organisational, and cultural issues.

Visions, goals, and objectives of an information-based university

This first section of an information strategy is the most important, in that it sets the strategic frame for the specific institutional focus of policies and investments concerning information resources (systems and infrastructure).

Strategy link

As mentioned earlier, the information strategy should be clearly linked to the institutional strategy. How is information processing and information technology expected to contribute to the achievements of the overall institutional goals and objectives? How does the institution expect to gain competitive advantages (with regard to cost, quality of services, timeliness of services provided and "production processes", service orientation and meeting customer expectations) through the implementation and use of information technology, information systems and information policy? How does the institution manage to use IT efficiently, building on the synergetic effects of IT, using the integrative potential of IT?

In this section, the institutional information strategy should provide a clear vision of what is expected to be achieved with the implementation and use of information technology and information systems.

Information systems: the "glue" of the organisation

This part of an information strategy refers to the importance of information for an organisation. It provides the managerial and leadership view of the use of information for organisational integrity, and for the match between central concerns and decentralisation patterns of a university. It makes clear that information is taken seriously in the context of decision-making, of quality and performance improvement, and of reporting and accountability duties.

The more institutional autonomy an institution is granted, the more it has to rely on information for decision-making, problem solving , and controlling activities. A self-reflective university should also have some knowledge about itself: "Universities are pre-eminently knowledge producing and transmitting institutions. Should they also not have within themselves the capacity to collect and analyse information about their institutional functioning including their success in teaching and research and all the other things they do?" (Martin Trow).

This section shows how the institution intends to cope with these informational challenges the university is facing. Also, for contract management, with governments and other funders (*e.g.* research funding agencies), for pricing decisions and internal allocation, valid information is needed. Reporting, marketing, and public relations are other areas of information use, and it seems important that an institution acknowledges the strategic importance of this kind of information use, and finds ways to handle this kind of information comprehensively and as efficient as possible through IT.

In a decentralised organisation, shared information may contribute to a corporate identity, to shared visions and values, and to co-ordination of decentralised decisions. Information systems may provide the institutional memory, and make of an information-based organisation a learning organisation (not only an organisation of learners). Institutional information systems, be they devoted to institutional or public electronic access, play an increasingly important role. This part of the information strategy might show, for an external public and an internal audience, that these are the items an institutional information policy consists of, and that this is the role information and information systems, with the support of information technology, are expected to play.

Access

It is very important for an institutional information strategy to clarify who should participate in the information, information systems and information technology, who to encourage to participate, or to whom the facilities are to be made accessible. Who should benefit from the investments in information resources, who should be served?

Questions of access have at least two dimensions: the contents of the information, and the physical access, in the sense of using hardware and software. The first touches problems of confidentiality, privacy, security, evaluation, and control. It is the question of an information policy that is to be solved and clarified in the information strategy. The second includes questions of charging or free of charge access, of student-owned computing and network services for private and computer facilities of staff and students. With regard to access one might differentiate

- *who:* department and central administration, managers and staff, academics and students, university members and the public; and

- *from where:* from the offices, from the classrooms, from private homes and dormitories, from public places within the institution, from the public in general, *e.g.* via videotex, Internet, telephone, fixed or mobile.

Commitment for infrastructure and innovation

An institutional information strategy should also make clear that there is a shared commitment within the institution; that the institution's task fulfilment and services rely on an ever up-to-date IT infrastructure; that the re-investments needed maintain the infrastructure are well planned and unquestioned; that the organisation is reviewed and adapted if necessary in order to be adequate for this purpose. Also, the institution should show what kind of role it intends to play with regard to innovating leading-edge use of information technology and how it guarantees that an appropriate share of the budget is devoted (top-sliced) to this purpose, and to what extent a free-of-charge use of IT is planned for innovation. The distinction of mature and innovative IT is a relative one, and it is at the discretion of an individual institution to establish a dividing-line. This, however, should be clarified in the information strategy of the respective institution.

Information culture

One of the essential elements of an infrastructure, which supports the efficient and effective use of information for the purpose of achieving institutional goals, has been identified in this paper as being the organisational culture of an institution. In this context, this cultural element of shared visions, assumptions, and behaviour of institutional members is called: *the information culture.* Culture is a more complex, sensitive and elusive matter, as is an investment in technology. And, culture cannot simply be made, as can an investment through the devotion of a certain amount of money and the selection process of a specific piece of software or hardware among the possible alternatives. Culture might rather emerge through the success institutional members experience, based on the specific assumptions and behaviour they share. But, culture is also a result of leadership activity, and the institutional information is strategy to a certain extent a leadership activity.

An institutional information strategy should clarify what is expected from the institutional members and how they should feel guided, encouraged, and empowered towards meeting these expectations. What is information culture? Four traits characterise an information culture:

- *Commitment to information sharing.* With a living commitment to information sharing, the first question is not whether an information should be shared with others in the organisation, but rather whether it should not be shared. Admittedly, there are touchy information pieces that are being generated in the course of the production processes and the evaluation of the outcomes and the quality of the performances. But, the commitment to sharing information is embedded in a deeply-rooted service orientation, and the organisational model of horizontal (in contrast to hierarchical) co-ordination and feedback, where the exchange of information, apart from exchange of services, plays the eminent role. This is the self-co-ordinating model of higher education, which heavily relies on information exchange. Sharing information implies also that there is the prevailing belief and assumption that shared values and commitment for the all organisation level tasks, and image and performance are s to be achieved beyond partial benefits, and that this is only achievable if there is a free exchange of information within the organisation. Commitment for information sharing also means that there is a strive for clarity, transparency and decisions based on information.

- *Acceptance of standards.* Information may be rich and anecdotal. It may be qualitative and differentiated. But, especially for decisions-making by the institutions, or decisions the clients and funders have to make with regard to their demand or allocation choices, information has to be presented in a comparable and a standardised form, where quantitative elements are as important as narrative qualitative elements. Acceptance of standards does not only refer to the contents of information, but also to information processing. There are many domains of information processing where the "not invented here" culture does not yield to efficiency and effectiveness gains while implementing and using IT. This might apply, for example, to administrative computing and computer-aided software.

- *Openness towards hands-on technology.* As mentioned earlier, there will always be some obstacles to the access and use of the tools and instruments, which necessarily play the role of intermediates between the end-user and the computerised information. Information culture means that these obstacles are not welcome, in order to refrain from computerised information handling at all, but rather are regarded as minor and manageable. If necessary, an institution with an information culture will devote extra funds and service staff to overcome these obstacles, instead of leaving the institutional members alone in their "fight" against technology.

- *Enthusiasm about innovations through information technology.* This implies that it is accepted that information technology may alter the fundamentals of the business of higher education, and that information technology may enable fundamental re-engineering of the primary and supporting processes in higher education.

Visions, goals, and objectives with regard to applications

Applications (information systems) should not be regarded as isolated entities, but as inter-related, as Figure 2.11 tries to visualise. They are inter-related, because the users have an integrated, common access (with regard to the various services under review). The systems use the same carrier, *i.e.* the campus network together with its links to the external network world, and finally all the applications directly or indirectly have to serve the same institutional goals and objectives, achieved with the aid of the information systems.

This part of the institutional information strategy will exemplify the visions, goals, and objectives of each of the application domains, and it will show the inter-relationships between them, and explain how the systems implemented or planned contribute to the achievement of the institutional goals and objectives.

Administration

The main aim of the administrative computing systems is not to serve the administration, the clerks, but rather to improve the services the administration is supposed to provide for the institutional members. What the administration provides, are mainly information services, and even if it follows only rules and regulations (*e.g.* with the accounting system), the potential of these systems will have to be revealed and used with regard to the services for the primary processes in higher education and research (*e.g.* use of accounting systems for the calculation of research projects in the application phase). This part of the information strategy should also show how information systems for administrative purposes may contribute to re-engineering the administrative processes (*e.g.* support the collaboration between service recipient, decentralised administration and central administration).

Management/institutional information systems

In this part, it will have to be shown how information systems do not only serve the top-management, wherever this may be located within a higher education institution, but what it means in practice: information sharing in a flat, professional, self-organising organisation, such as the higher education institution. It will develop the path from an Executive Information System to an Enterprise Information System (EIS).

Public relations/accountability/marketing

In this part, it is necessary to take into account that much of the information that is needed in the PR and accountability context is already available in other (*e.g.* administrative) contexts. It is therefore essential that the efficiency of information processing, the reduction of information costs, is achieved through IT. These applications rely heavily on the institutional information policy, *i.e.* the question solved what kind of information should be shared internally and externally.

Teaching/learning

As an example of what can be explained in this part of the information strategy with regard to the applications for teaching and learning support the case of California Polytec is used as a reference (see Baker and Gloster, 1994). Cal Poly's goals, with regard to the teaching and learning applications, are based on the assumption that information technology may benefit learning:

- it allows a student to take a more active role;
- allows the teacher to express the content of a course in more than one format;
- broadens the array of resources brought to a classroom or the student's   workstations;
- increases the opportunities for interaction between teacher and student and   for interaction among students;
- reduces barriers to university services; and
- increases the productivity of those who support the learning environment.

The four goals for an electronic campus which serve teaching and learning are:

- a networked instructional environment, based on universal e-mail, shared information resources, and computerised classrooms;
- easy access to workstations and networked information services;
- institutional support for faculty and student development of computer-based communication skills; and
- simplified interfaces, procedures and documentation for accessing networked   information services.

Research

IT for research is to a great extent the focus of decentralised decisions based on visions, missions, goals and perspectives of the respective units and individuals within the institution. But, there is a need for co-ordination and shared perspectives, especially with regard to the infrastructure common to all the different users, especially the network and the access to the services that are only available through the access to international networks and information systems. An attractive IT environment might endow the institution with competitive advantage in the course of attracting outstanding researchers.

Information services/library

This section about applications might show the path towards the virtual library, and on-demand publishing for the institutional members. It might show how IT may lead to reduction of space needed and thus to cost reduction.

Communication

The electronic communication facilities (communication systems) may have impacts with regard to the services the institution intends to provide, and the clientele it wishes to have. This section might demonstrate how far the institution intends to use IT to change services and clientele (electronic campus, distance learning, virtual university).

Infrastructure -- Implementation

This third part of the information strategy, referring to the infrastructure level of the three-layered concept of information management in higher education, eventually encompasses all the details of implementation of the previously-described visions, goals, and objectives. As mentioned above infrastructure includes technology, organisation, and cultural issues. Thus, this part of the information strategy will have to contain details concerning all three elements of an information resources infrastructure.

Technology

The technology part will have to explain all the details regarding investments, re-investments or de-investments concerning networks, external connectivity, central computing and other facilities, access, and user interfaces. Also the guidelines for decentral investments, as far as connecting to the campus network is intended, and as far as central services are intended to be provided, will have to be detailed.

Organisation

In this section of the information strategy, one will have to deal with the financing, re-investment, and operating expenditure issues that derive from the investment plans. External liaisons, co-operation issues, and the kind of central services to be provided will be considered. What services and IT facilities to be charged? What should be encouraged for use by a free-of-charge policy? By whom and how procurement decisions are to be made? These are additional issues that belong to this section. Finally, it should be made clear where and how the information strategy decisions are made.

Culture

As stated earlier, culture emerges. But, to a certain extent, it can be made through the activities of leaders, through measures and mechanisms. This section will show what kind of measures, means and mechanisms are being implemented, with the expectation to develop certain shared assumptions and behaviours that have been identified to characterise the information culture -- such as training, guidance and support facilities, central service units, service agreements with regard to these units, rewards, incentives structures and features, and funds, time-allocated for innovations, and experimentation and learning.

Conclusions

The underlying assumption is that information management is not only an issue for *functional management*, but for *general management* of higher education institutions (rectors, presidents, deans and department heads, chief administrators). Information management has been identified as focusing on three layers: information use and handling, information systems, and information resources infrastructure, inter-related through support and requirement links. Three challenges which higher education institutions face were identified: the informational challenge leading to a more demanding information processing in the primary (teaching and research) as well as in the managerial processes; the technological challenges, information technology bearing the potential in itself of revolutionising the higher education business as an information intensive business; and finally, the policy and financing challenge related to the IT issues, referring to major changes in this domain of higher education policy and financing. All these challenges together lead the institutions to develop an information strategy, based on the commitment of general institutional management, and which does not only focus on the basic level of the three layers, the IT infrastructure, but which is derived from the overall institutional strategy, and is lead by the idea that information processing, information systems and the information resources infrastructure may significantly contribute to the achievements of institutional goals and objectives.

REFERENCES

Baker, W.J. and Gloster II, A.S. (1994), "Moving towards the virtual university: a vision of technology in higher education", in CAUSE/EFFECT, Vol. 17, No. 2, Summer, pp. 4-11.

Barta, B. Z., Telem, M., and Gev, Y. (eds.) (1995), *Information Technology in Educational Management*, London.

Earl, M. J. (1989), *Management Strategies for Information Technology,* New York.

HEIR Alliance (1992), "What presidents need to know about the integration of information technologies on campus", HEIR Alliance Executive Strategies Report No. 1, September.

HEIR Alliance (1995), "Evaluation guidelines for institutional information resources", CAUSE, Boulder, Colorado.

Orna, E. (1990), Practical Information Policies: How to Manage Information Flows in Organizations, London.

Press, L. (1994), "Tomorrow's campus", in CACM, Vol. 37, No. 7, pp. 13-17, July.

Wollnick, M. (1998), "Ein Referenzmodell des Informations Management", in *Information Management,* Vol. 3, pp. 34-43.

Figure 2.1. **Information management layers**

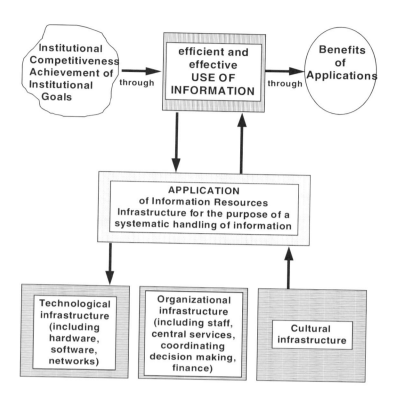

Figure 2.2. **Exchange process model of higher education**

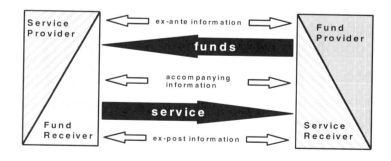

Figure 2.3. **Information based exchange processes in higher education**

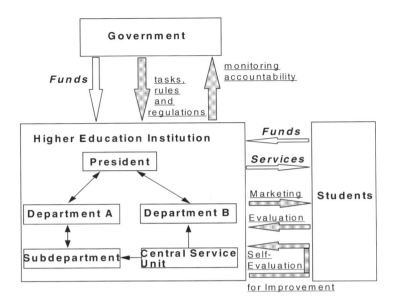

Figure 2.4. **Interdependence**

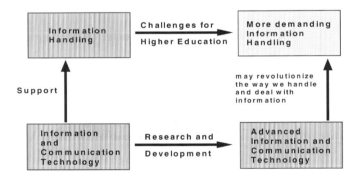

Figure 2.5. **SWOTS analysis**

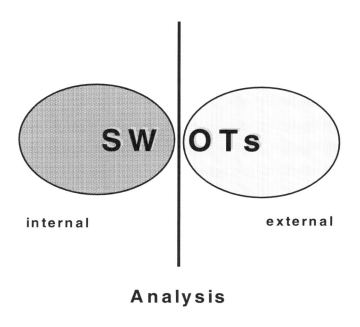

Figure 2.6. **Strengths and weaknesses analysis for an information strategy**

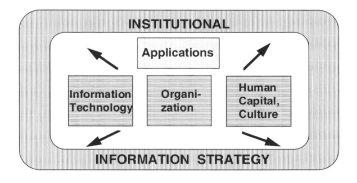

Figure 2.7. **Opportunities and threats analysis for an information strategy**

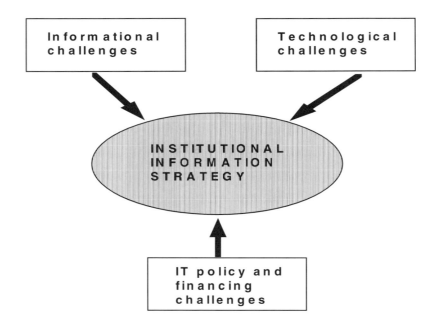

Figure 2.8. **The history of information management related strategies**

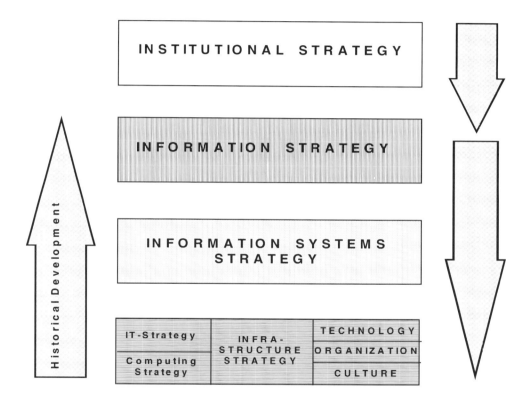

Figure 2.9. **The hierarchy of strategies**

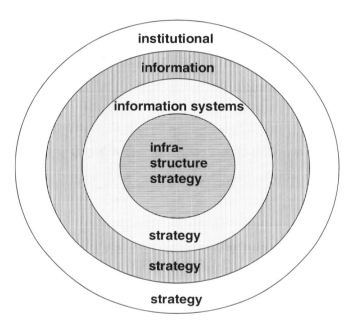

Figure 2.10. **Three-layered structure of an information strategy**

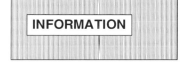

INFORMATION

Visions, Goals, and
Objectives of an
Information Based
University

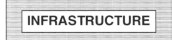

**INFORMATION
SYSTEMS**

Visions, Goals, and
Objectives with
regard to Applications

INFRASTRUCTURE

Implementation:

- technological
- organizational
- cultural

Figure 2.11. **Institutional applications of the information resources infrastructure**

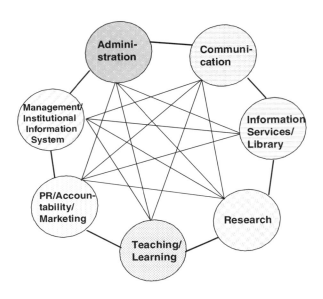

- common access
- common carrier
- common institutional goals to be achieved

Chapter 3

FINANCING, BUDGETING, AND CHARGING PROBLEMS RELATED TO INFORMATION TECHNOLOGY IN HIGHER EDUCATION

by

Edgar Frackmann

Introduction

As part of the IMHE project "Information Management -- Information Technology as an Emerging Issue for Institutional Management in Higher Education", a workshop of experts in the field has been organised focusing on the financing, budgeting, and charging problems related to information technology in higher education. Whatever activity is undertaken, whatever information technology policy is to be implemented in higher education, funds must be devoted to this purpose, resources deployed and allocated, and financial decisions made. As soon as the first results of the IMHE project were presented to an interested audience (institutional managers), the request that the project team continue the project arose, emphasizing the financial issues of information technology in higher education.

During the course of the workshop, the participants quickly came to the conclusion that issues of financing and financing mechanisms could be discussed both in terms of other equipment and facilities in higher education, like buildings, scientific equipment, and laboratories, and that the issues involved would perhaps not differ in a significant way from another. Dealing with financial issues -- this was the result of these considerations -- means not only asking where the money should come from and how it should be allocated to those who claim to need it. In the case of IT, it instead means dealing with information policy, the role of information technology in this context, the changing environment and characteristics of information technology, setting priorities, and questions of efficiency, effectiveness, and institutional culture. To put it succinctly, the issue of financing, chosen as one of the expert workshops in the IMHE project, turned out to focus most comprehensively on the core issues of institutional management in higher education concerning information technology.

Information technology in higher education is not an aim in itself, nor are investments in IT made simply for the sake of IT. Rather, IT is a means to use, handle, access, and transfer information. Due to the potential of information technology, however, the way in which this is or can be done may alter, if not revolutionise, the role of information in society and in our daily working and leisure life. Higher education and research, as an information intensive enterprise, and an enterprise dealing with the future of societies (in educating the future workforce and in inventing and developing future technology), may be one of the first societal institutions to cope with this new role of information technology. And financing questions, the core of management and policy issues related to information technology, must be addressed based on these more general considerations about the information society, and the changing role and characteristics of information technology.

The underlying structure for the considerations in this paper will thus start by dealing with the information society in the information age, and higher education and research in this context. The challenges facing higher education related to information technology, IT policy, and financing IT, will follow these more general contentions. Policy and management issues will be dealt with in a subsequent section, followed by a discussion of the main issues, trends, and tendencies related to financing IT in higher education. The final section, a summary and conclusion, will be devoted to recommendations for institutional management.

The information society -- The information age

The information society

Characteristics and developments in society and organisations today leave no doubt that future society will be an information society. The corporation, or in more general terms, the organisation, will be based less on hierarchy, location, and space than on sharing information, regardless of its location or the location of those people involved in the organisation, where flat structures with smaller units, if not individuals, take on full information responsibilities. Competitive nations and organisations will be those which can succeed in creating the "learning organisation", where not only physical commodities and production, but also how information and knowledge are generated and handled, will form the underlying organising principles. To be competitive in terms of cost, time, quality, and service, will mean that corporations and organisations organise information handling and information links in the most efficient and effective possible manner. The future society will be based on virtual organisations built on shared information, goals, and values, on a co-operative creation of knowledge and information, rather than simply location or physical proximity and production.

The role and characteristics of information technology

Information technology in its present stage has the potential to revolutionise the way people handle and deal with information. Humanity seems to be living in an historical period similar to the time when printing was invented. Three characteristics can be identified, which contribute to this revolutionary role of information technology:

1) High speed information highways with merging technologies and converging information channels. Data processing no longer represents the core benefits of information technology, but rather the transfer of information in whatever form (multimedia). The network is the system.

2) The development of user friendly, flexible, mobile, intelligent access tools with end-user conformed retrieval, filtering, selection, and conversion facilities. Every individual can thus become a data-processing node in an overall organisational and world-wide networked system.

3) The accessibility of information wherever it is needed, independent of its location, information which may represent the shared "memory" of an organisation (information sharing organisation).

These characteristics give information technology an enabling function, a leverage function for the information society, for the flat, knowledge-based, learning organisation -- to put it succinctly -- for the competitive organisation and the competitive nation.

To develop information technology, to invest in IT infrastructure, ranging from the network to IT literacy of the future work force and citizen, thus has an economic relevance not only for the development of the IT industry, but for the whole national economy and its enterprises. Like roads, railways, or airline connections in the past, today the IT infrastructure must be regarded as the backbone and main building block of future economic development, wealth, and competitiveness. And like past investments in infrastructure, IT investments are the focus of a mixture of public and private financial endeavours and decision-making.

At the same time, there are two problematic issues to be considered in dealing with the role of IT in economic development:

– As is usually the case with infrastructure for the economy, it might take some prior initiative from the public purse and policy, some push and encouragement of innovation before private initiative and financing can carry on alone.

– While information technology might reach a certain degree of development, the business world may fail to take it up because the market is yet to be developed and matured to the extent that investment in this latest stage of technology seems attractive to private investors. In terms of IT and some aspects of its future development and implementation (multi-media, merging of technologies, broad-band transmission), entertainment and short-term consumption seem to be the driving force. Public policy might have to take some corrective activity to encourage the development and implementation of IT for the productive, learning, and democratic society independent of the pace dictated by the market for entertainment and short-term consumption.

Information technology in higher education and research

Three terms can be used to characterise the relationship between higher education and research and IT: innovation, efficiency, and information society.

Innovation

Higher education plays a clearly innovative role in information technology. Above all, higher education and research have the task of producing information in the form of new knowledge, and to transfer it to both students and the audience of the research community. Information technology is not only a focus of research in higher education, but with its primary task in mediating information and knowledge, higher education should apply the latest innovative technology: especially students, the future workforce, need to be acquainted with the technology of the future early in their educational careers. Even if researchers in higher education do not always invent the latest technology (but sometimes have to leave this privilege to industry's research laboratories), they might be the first to use it in a new or comprehensive way, before it is marketable and profitable for industry. For the implementation and use of IT in higher education and research, the development of knowledge, culture, and the development of a learning society might be the driving forces, rather than entertainment. The higher education and research community can act as the "testing-ground" for the latest technology, a field of transfer to industry and society as a whole. In this sense, the development of information technology in higher education and research might become high priority in national policies on research, development, and infrastructure. Given its innovative role in this context, it is important that higher education institutions are receptive to close contacts and co-operation with industry.

Efficiency

Information technology, whether applied in higher education or elsewhere, has a service function. One of the most important services is to enhance the efficiency of the information-based work at hand. Since higher education's primary task is to deal with information, one of the most important aims of implementing information technology in higher education should be to increase the efficiency of its own work. When applying for IT-related funds, higher education can argue that it can significantly increase its own efficiency. Electronically-stored information, for example, can save a great deal of the space needed for libraries. Electronic access to information and electronic communication can save time and travelling expenses. More extensive use of CBI can help reduce the space and personnel-related expenditure of a higher education institution. Computer support for administration and management can reduce the time and personnel devoted to administration and decision-making. Teachers and researchers in higher education could do their jobs more efficiently because of the wide-spread implementation and use of information technology.

Information society

Peter Drucker, in an article about the coming of the new organisation, contended that the future business organisation might show more characteristics of an orchestra, hospital, or university. These organisations are characterised by flat structures, co-operation of experts based on the development and exchange of knowledge, information responsibility at the organisation base, with a loose and temporary goal-oriented coupling of organisational subunits (adhocracy), with open boundaries and independent of location (virtual organisation). Some of the above aspects, what Drucker classified as inherent to university organisation, admittedly reflect the reality of universities only in an idealised way. But, universities may develop into information societies, into global, virtual, location-independent international organisations, based on unlimited exchange of information in whatever form, due to the leverage function of information technology. The potential of today's state-of-the-art information technology exists and needs only to be implemented more comprehensively. The handling of information in the scientific community has reached or has the potential to reach a new stage. Information technology may revolutionise the activities and thus effectiveness of higher education and research.

Information technology and finance: challenges for higher education

Financing information technology involves governments, self-organising (buffer) organisations, and finally institutional management to an equal extent. All find themselves today in a specific situation regarding information technology and its financing. This section will attempt to characterise this situation by listing the main challenges that conceivably face higher education and its financing bodies.

Importance of information technology

Information technology in higher education is important, not only for the role it may play as described in the previous paragraphs, but also for its wide-spread existence in higher education institutions and its share in the overall institutional budget.

Information technology has already spread to every facet of the whole higher education and research process, ranging from the primary processes of teaching, learning, and research, to supporting processes like administration and information supply and communication. It has created expectations and dependencies, as well as gains in efficiency, which cannot be neglected in planning for re-investment within the institutional budget. A more or less generous investment in information technology cannot simply mean to "bump equipment" into higher education institutions. To the same if not greater extent, one has to consider software, maintenance personnel, and finally connections (the share of institutional and overall network and communication costs), which all increase the value of the equipment beyond mere data processing. The space for equipment might be another significant factor in such calculations, even when information technology contributes to space-saving in other respects.

Due to the amount of funds dedicated to reinvestment in information technology, higher education institutions risk running short on investment funds for innovation. Moreover, a tendency toward short-term investment may come at the expense of long-term and infrastructural provisions.

Changing structure of information technology

A dramatic change in information technology has made an impact on financing and investment. During the mainframe era, institutions needed a big chunk of money for reinvestment every 8 to 10 years. Today, a continuous flow of money is needed to keep wide-spread smaller units up-to-date. An increasing share of these investment decisions are made decentrally rather than centrally, as was the case for mainframes. As a consequence, IT money is increasingly taken from departmental and other institutional subunits' budgets. Follow-up costs, like software and personnel, are often underestimated in these decentralised budget decisions. And, short-term special-interest decisions tend to be made on the expense of infrastructural decisions.

Infrastructure has taken on another sense over the course of IT development. In the mainframe age, infrastructure meant that institutional members should simply have access to central computing capacities, and at times not even direct access to the work place. Today, IT-infrastructure has two facets. One facet is represented by computing power and communication access as close as possible to the individual end user. This side of IT infrastructure is often the result of many decentralised decisions and budget priorities, and only partially the focus of central initiative and finance. The other increasingly important facet of IT infrastructure is the network, the institutional network and access to national research and international networks. Networking costs are the source of the most visible financial problems for higher education. The costs are increasing exponentially as transmission speed is upgraded from 9.6 kbit, 64 kbit, 2 Mbit, 34 Mbit, 140 Mbit, to Gigabits etc. This is one of the most pressing financial problems for higher education in its goal to play an innovative, pilot role in the future of the information society. How can politicians be convinced that the price of this program for higher education and research is not too high ?

Phases of information technology development and implementation

Components of information technology go through a life cycle, at least in theory. In practice, however, especially for management decisions, it is very difficult to determine the moments of transition from one phase to the next.

There are at least two major phases to be distinguished in order to delineate different management decisions about financing. The first is the innovation phase. Society at large might lag behind technological possibilities, *i.e.* IT is further developed than its actual use. Universities might take on innovative and pilot user-role, or higher education and research can serve as a testing-ground for certain technologies. The exploratory use of new technology has to be encouraged. Charging for use would be detrimental to this purpose. Innovative budgets and promotional funding are financial means to achieve this goal. Innovative budgets are an essential part of this vision for certain newly-developed components of information technology.

The other phase is the phase of maturity. A specific IT component is well established and well accepted. Its use might even explode and cause severe problems in resource provisions, even when such use is billed. However, the IT component may well belong to an infrastructure which has to be available, even if not fully used all the time (*i.e.* telephone). When use (for things) like network services is exploding, it is very difficult to distinguish between play and research, leisure and work. On the other hand, it is not difficult to imagine how much time is spent " gophering ", or "webbing", when the individual user is not billed. In the phase of maturity, the financial means for providing IT is operational funding. IT aims to achieve efficient and effective work in higher education and research. Charging for use can be based on a range of roughly-measured user shares. Users are provided not only with technology, as was the case in the innovative phase, but can themselves decide if and to what extent they want to use IT resources, and can set their own (budgetary) priorities.

In reality, however, it is difficult to make such a distinction between innovation and infrastructure (maturity). National-level decision-makers and institutional managers find themselves between Scylla and Charybdis. They see IT, especially networks either over or under-used. They do not believe that higher education and research really need 34 Mbit, and they complain that the network in its present stage is abused. They do not know whether to encourage use or to place a price on services. IT-related self-organising bodies (see below) could help institutional and national higher education managers to make appropriate, well-informed decisions.

Visibility of costs

Once a technology has been provided free-of-charge, in order to promote its use and encourage innovation, people often take it for granted and the cost structure remains almost invisible. This may in turn cause severe problems, if the distinction and transition between the innovation and maturity phase has to be managed. There are two other problems with IT cost in higher education. One is that follow-up costs are not fully taken into account. One needs to consider not only investment in equipment but software as well. The software share of IT budgets tends to exceed hardware costs by far. Underestimating software cost might result in illegal software use, nor is the personnel cost for installing, connecting to the network, operating and maintaining hardware and software often made really visible enough. The other problem is that, traditionally, higher education is organised on a decentral basis. IT today supports this decentralisation and apart from the networking infrastructure, the bulk of investments is determined decentrally. As a result hidden costs, duplication of work and experience (if not to say costly trial and error) are not easily captured, and avoided in the flat organisation of higher education institutions. On the other hand, a cost accounting system, able to offer a realistic picture of all IT costs, and able to help manage this considerable share of an institution's overall budget, can itself be very expensive.

Managing growth

IT use, implementation, and share of institutional budget still need to grow, in view of the development towards the information society and the pilot role of higher education. There is a tremendous need for reinvestment due to the overall spread of IT to work in the higher education and research, and to extend the use of IT, and improve networking speed and capacity. During periods of economic crisis, budgets for higher education and research are often reduced. Managing growth in a situation of countervailing forces has at least four dimensions:

- *Promoting more efficient use of existing IT resources and funds for IT.* This may mean more co-ordination and resource-sharing throughout the institution by using central services, accepting standards instead of lobby for special status, and accepting and enhancing the visibility of cost and cost structures.

- *Deliberate use of IT to enhance efficiency*, in order to show that IT can act as a leverage for other budget items and to achieve gains in efficiency.

- *Convincing funders and sponsors* that those in higher education and research can be innovative promotional users of new technology, and that this can contribute to overall national economic and social improvement.

- *Seeking other funding sources*, especially while co-operating and sharing resources with partners from the corporate world and national enterprises.

National policies

Especially in publicly-funded higher education systems, IT is heavily dependent on national policy and available public funds. This always holds for the initial and innovation phase of networking, and its subsequent development in transmission speed and capacity. IT budgets are flexible in the worst sense, vulnerable to fluctuations in public funds for higher education. In the past, the main focus of national policy and financial initiatives was on big projects, such as computing centres, high performance computing, and networks. Only to a certain extent did these national programs follow the downsizing of computing facilities towards the infrastructural, wide-spread distribution and provision of computing facilities, such as computers for students or for scholarly purpose. There is an overall trend from national seed money to total user-funding out of their general budgets. The danger clearly exists that the necessary funding for IT innovation, which still necessary in higher education and research, especially in networking, will run short.

National governments are accustomed to promoting IT in higher education and research for the sake of the country's IT industry. But, there are other compelling reasons for government initiative and funding. More than technology itself, the revolutionised use of information merits attention, and the development towards the competitive information society makes it valuable for governments to invest in higher education IT. And, higher education could develop and realise the visions of the information society.

Institutional information strategy

Institutions and their subunits must become used to establishing their own priorities, deciding more deliberately whether or not to emphasize a certain degree of IT implementation. In other words, institutions need an information strategy. Indeed this strategy starts with the information problem. Where previously one dealt with IT in terms of using technology, IT is now related to the technology-enabled use of information. What information is needed and where within the institution? How does one avoid duplication of input, storage, or purchase of information? How does one avoid wasted space? How does one plug into external information sources most efficiently and effectively? How can one integrate information and communication channels in a cost effective manner?

An IT strategy needs to address decision-making, financing, and charging issues. Central services are offered to allow decentralised units to participate in a more cost-effective use of IT-related budget shares at their discretion. Charging might be necessary for one or the other infrastructural IT facility or central service. These charging and budgeting procedures need to be simple and easy enough so that they do not become another source of administrative overhead and cost.

IT-related policies and management issues

The considerations thus far underscore the following three main changes in IT in higher education:

- IT consists of smaller units, in terms of price and space needed, and these units tend to be located close to individual members of an institution.

- The IT infrastructure is the network, *i.e.* the subunits LAN, campus network, national research network, and connection to international networks.

- In terms of information technology, technology is no longer the issue. Policy and management need to pay attention to issues such as handling information, access to information, and communication issues.

There is no question that these changes have consequences for policies and management activities. They can effect three levels, especially regarding the policies and activities closely related to financing: government, self-organising bodies, and institutional management.

The changing role of government

Government policies often tend to be influenced by general financial restrictions or a relative "abundance" of public funds. Financial crises in public funds, due to overall national economic problems, can mean that the big IT programmes which benefited higher education and research in the past, become rare.

To a certain extent, however, another rationale is at work behind this current lack of large investment programs. If IT infrastructure means installing computers everywhere and for every person, there is then rather a need for continuous investment and re-investment than a big bulk investment every ten years. It could, of course, be a policy goal or focus of a government financial initiative to advance a "computers everywhere and for every person in higher education" infrastructure with seed money or large allocations of funds. In general, however, decisions about what to spend on this front-end part of IT infrastructure could be left to decentralised units, and these allocations can be "hidden" in general budgets of institutions and their subunits, which can use their own discretion about priorities and the pace of investment and reinvestment. Governments do not need to conduct an itemised discussion with institutions, but rather to listen to institutions' overall plans and information strategy. Despite these considerations, a potential for national programs remains, which is summarised as follows:

Campus network

Not all the institutions have a campus network. Even in cases where a campus network is in place, there is still the next step towards networks that allow multimedia transmission and external access. The campus network is still an infrastructural effort of the institution as a whole, where the necessary and immediate allocation of funds might have to come from special state or national programs and support.

National research network

In many countries, the national research network has reached the stage of maturity, with a transmission speed of 9.6 kbit or 64 kbit, but has yet to realise speeds of 2 Mbit or 34 Mbit or more. The research networks are far below the level of allowing multimedia transmission, and the implementation of ATM technology is still in its infancy. Higher education and research may act as a testing-ground for these new technologies and for applications based on new technologies.

International connectivity

In certain cases, using international networks is more expensive than the carrier within national boundaries. Education and research, however, are global undertakings, and researchers need international connectivity. This might well be a field not only for national sponsoring, but of international negotiations undertaken by national governments or their European counterparts.

Information services including libraries

The electronic support and provision of information is still in a stage which can be called the innovation phase, and could well need national funding. The organisation, co-ordination, and financing of developments in this field could still be a field of national activity, including the following:

- setting up and maintaining databases for education and research or access to international databases;

- development of standards (common record format for information beyond the national domain);

- support for developments in on-demand publishing and electronic document and article delivery, including copyright problems;

55

– support for the development of navigational tools;

– support for the retrospective conversion of catalogues into electronic readable form; and

– promoting the implementation of library automation and management systems.

Applications

The revolution in handling information has become more important than just implementing and promoting technology to support each nation's technology production. In higher education, technology can be used in many aspects of the teaching and learning process, and national programs could do much to promote these applications. Developing educational software fails to come under a well-established culture of co-ordinating educational activities and reputation through software development. National programs and financial incentives could help stimulate the educational IT applications and develop this missing culture.

The changing role of self-organising bodies

Self-organising bodies are located between governments and the scientific community. Their academic orientation is usually strong, since they consist of experts from the academic community who are recruited by academics themselves. Their previous role, however, was of a clearly political nature, to process requests from the academic community on government bodies. The government expected them to allocate IT-related funds to higher education and research, and to develop IT policy for government. As is often the case with intermediaries, the policies developed by such self-organising bodies, as the British or the German Computer Board, had two sides. On the one hand, the computer-recommendation board served to direct the public funds along a consistent policy, and IT development on the national level, at the expense of some institutional fund applications. On the other hand, their policy recommendations encouraged institutions, and provided backup for their IT investment applications, even in cases where they diverged from national or state financial possibilities and priorities.

The IT-related buffer organisations had two transmission functions clearly dependent on finances:

– *The transmission function down to institutions, their subunits, and researchers.* In both allocating funds, in accordance with their policies, and judging applications of institutions and researchers (*i.e.* accepting or rejecting the applications), this functioned in a "downwards" direction and inevitably showed some "bureaucratic" traits.

– *The transmission function upwards to politicians can be characterised as policy advice and policy-making.* It seems evident that many national IT programs for higher education and research have been launched by these self-organising bodies.

Today, the IT-related intermediary bodies are on verge of a significant change in their role. These modifications refer back to the transmission functions mentioned thus far. As stated earlier, governments can allocate funds to IT without becoming involved in an item-by-item discussion of the many small units that nowadays characterise one side of the IT infrastructure. Thus, governments no longer need outside advice in this respect. More important is the overall institutional IT plan based on the institutional information strategy. This is more a concern of the individual institution than of government, so that the various bits of centrally and decentrally decided IT units fit into an overall strategy.

Self-organising bodies may thus have to shift their attention and advice from governments to institutions. Institutions could seek recommendations from IT-related buffer bodies, who could provide guidance to institutions, including advice about institutional IT plans and information strategies, indicators and controlling systems to help monitor effective and efficient use of IT, indicators to provide information about the use level of IT resources, indicators to help develop an IT investment policy, organisation and management of IT resources and information systems, procurement strategies, security standards and measures, and model contract terms for externally provided IT services.

Intermediary bodies are increasingly taking on the role of self-organising bodies for higher education institutions. They can no longer rely on their relationship to computing centre heads or eminent researchers in computer science, but need to build a relationship with the institution's most senior managers. These bodies maintain a policy function towards government. They promote the need for public investment in the IT infrastructure for higher education and research, and for the information society as a whole. This policy function embraces networking, libraries and information systems, super-computing, and new technologies such as parallel systems software development, multi-media, and knowledge-based systems.

The new self-organising bodies also have a co-ordination function for institutions, to provide co-ordination and co-operation where joint efforts raise efficiency and effectiveness, and lower costs for IT components. They can secure special rate software licences for higher education and research. They can even organise joint software development (*i.e.* for administrative computing or for computer-based instruction), and promote and organise joint research about new technology and its uses in such areas as teaching and learning.

Self-organising bodies can also be organised and work like service corporations, to administer public funds and membership, or users' fees, while providing certain services for higher education and research. These services may include the national research network, standard software, computing centres, and super-computers.

In the new IT era, institutions have more responsibility for their own IT infrastructure while public money for this purpose is at the same time becoming tighter. In order to benefit from experiences made elsewhere, to benefit from efficiency gains through co-ordination and co-operation, and to promote an IT infrastructure transcending the individual institution, self-organising bodies need to be "owned" by institutions rather than government.

The changing role of institutional management

In the mainframe era, institutional management, regardless of the level of the institution, had only one partner apart from government in dealing with planning, financing, investment, and re-investment of IT. Whatever the issue, decisions could be made over long cycles, and IT-related changes came to occur the in long term only. Institutional managers could leave it to computing centre heads to propose IT policy and to secure the "smooth operation" of both central resources and IT infrastructure.

Today, IT-relevant decisions are made at so many places within the institution that neither the computing centre head nor institutional managers can keep up with them. Institutional subunits have their own budgets, and they can reach independent decisions about if and when to invest in IT. Indeed, institutional management and computer centres might be tempted to leave the development of the institution's IT infrastructure up to the decisions of the various subunits.

However, IT infrastructure consists of more than the bits and pieces of desk top computing resources. Rather, it is a co-operative distributed processing with inter and intra-institutional connectivity. Beyond the individual desk, it needs IT infrastructure and central services. The vision of the information society, moreover, will not be achieved only by computer hardware in researchers' offices and student homes, but in institutional, national and international services on the network as well. Finally, the goals of efficient and effective use of IT-related resources will not be realised without co-operation, co-ordination, and joint efforts to avoid duplication and organise resource sharing. The role of institutional management in IT and financing IT can be subsumed under four headings: 1) visions and strategy, 2) organisation, 3) financing, and 4) institutional IT policy in external relations.

Visions and strategy

Individuals within the institution might have a vision of the information society and its realisation in the institution, but they also need to be able to influence institutional management and convince institutional management to share their goals. The information society vision could include constant access for every member of the institution to an array of network services, *i.e.* institutional information systems and access to national and international information systems and communication channels.

The vision might rely on a concept of information that implies all forms and media (multi-media) and facilitating access for everyone, not only for computer scientists. It may also focus on significant changes in teaching and learning methods due to IT. The latest technology should always be available within the institutional realm, at least in central pools and with central servers. The managerial vision, however, needs to include implementation policies, and the persuasion of institutional members, and foster behaviours and cultures which allow the vision to become reality. It also means developing plans and strategies, detecting gaps in efficiency, helping optimise available resources, and raising funds. The institutional strategy has dimensions such as organisation, financing, and external relations.

Organisation

- Responsibility structure

The procedures and organisational provisions for how IT equipment is purchased, operated, maintained, and reinvested have simply followed the changing structure of IT components without an overall plan. Although decentralisation might be welcomed by most participants, the result of this organisational development is, in many respects, far from ideal. The responsibility structure often remains ill-defined. Who is responsible (including financial responsibility) for purchasing, standards, follow-up costs like software, maintenance, software upgrading, operating support, user support and counselling, space, and other areas? In spite of the many decentralised computing facilities "on desk" and "in the bags" of institutional members, central (infrastructural resources need to be maintained and reinvested, such as networks, servers, and latest technology pools), and central services need to be offered for the sake of overall institutional efficiency and savings.

- Efficiency

In view of the contradiction between shrinking budgets and the need for IT investments to grow in order to develop the competitive information society, it is necessary to identify and realise all the means to improve the efficiency of IT use. With the integration of information systems, for example, it is important to avoid duplicating keyboarding effort, to save physical space with electronic handling of information, to reduce time and personnel, and to use resources efficiently with the integration of telephone and data transmission. Cost-tracking systems and performance indicators to monitor expenditures for IT, and the use of IT, can be very useful in order to become more efficient, both through IT and in using IT resources in a more efficient way.

But cost-tracking systems tend to be expensive, and themselves create administrative and data input overhead. This is especially true for IT costs, both because IT is located centrally and decentrally, and because there are many costs hidden by those who do not want to change existing organisational patterns. There are thus cases where it is not worthwhile to invest in costly cost-tracking systems, and to wait until they reveal what seems evident from the beginning: certain routine services like hardware and software installation, user services, maintenance, procurement including software licences, and centrally-offered services, are less expensive than providing them at places scattered throughout institutions. It might be wise simply to offer these services at a reasonable (cost covering) price to decentralised units, rather than to convince users with a costly cost-accounting system.

- Central services

One can distinguish between routine and strategic central services. While routine central services can include user service, installation, and maintenance of decentralised and central facilities (including the network), connecting computing units to campus network services and external network and information services, strategic services, on the other hand, are oriented towards more fundamental institutional information strategies and IT policies. They focus on developing IT procurement strategies for the whole institution, negotiating special rates and campus software licences, developing strategies concerning outsourcing, and developing institutional information systems strategies.

- Corporate-wide information systems

The backbone of these central strategic services is the care and provision of institution-wide information systems. This includes management information systems, public relations information systems, access to scientific purpose information systems, including the library, CD-ROMs, and remote access through the network, and finally the communication infrastructure to connect users with information systems and to make them independent of location.

Financing

Institutional management has to consider financing, while dealing with an information strategy and IT plans. An overall financial plan in line with the IT plan is needed, a plan that first focuses on resources needed and managed by the computing centre. Even if the responsibility for certain IT items is distributed among decentralised units, their decentralised budgets need to fit into some coherent plan. The need for growing investments and reinvestments still exists. Institutional management will thus need to set priorities and detect where other budget items can be reduced in favour of IT, where IT otherwise helps economise. By the same token, institutional management has to find and implement ways to use available IT resources more efficiently and effectively. One means is to organise co-operation, creating commitment to standards, resource-sharing, and offering central services. Follow-up costs, especially personnel, software and reinvestment also need to be taken thoroughly into account when, deciding on an IT purchase, and it needs to be clear from the beginning which institutional budgets should be charged for follow-up costs.

Institutional management will need indicators to help make decisions, that is, indicators about a "normal" level of IT equipment for an institution, "normal" follow-up cost, and reinvestment cycles. The financial plan will have to ensure that the required infrastructure of institutional IT is protected and not damaged through short-term decentralised investments. A balance between investment in innovation and investment in infrastructure also needs to be maintained.

Charging for central IT services can be applied to encourage the efficient and effective use of IT resources. But charging runs the risk of impeding IT use, or, if central services are not working satisfactorily, that users try to help themselves, often at the expense of efficiency. Charging must thus be linked to a commitment to outstanding user-friendly central IT-related services. And charging must offer straight-forward incentives. If charging is applied instead of top-slicing, this needs to be figured into the budgets of an institution's decentralised units.

External relations

The self-organising bodies mentioned earlier cannot do their task of organising the common interest of higher education and research in the IT domain without the support of institutional management. Institutional managers have to transfer their information society visions to self-organising bodies and thus engage them in the political work, towards goals such as the virtual library, cheap access to international lines, access to information systems, special software license rates for higher education and research, high-speed national research networks for multi-media transmission, and the corporate network for higher education and research as a whole.

Managing contradictions

To sum up, one could say that the new role of institutional management is to realise the visions of an information society in higher education and research while striking a balance between contradictory tendencies. On the one hand, a growing proportion of funds is still needed for IT and information policies of higher education institutions. On the other hand, the budgets are becoming tighter and tighter, and not only funders but internal budget receivers must to be convinced that a well-planned and effective investment in IT is needed, and to apply the most efficient way of using

IT-related budgets. Individual users may have to give up their newly acquired independence in decision-making and self-service, to a certain extent, in order to choose the more efficient alternative of central IT service provision.

On one hand, it seems to be necessary to promote new technology and encourage institutional users to work with new technology. This might best be achieved by not charging for IT use. On the other hand, in order to improve the service level of central service providers and achieve a thoughtful use of IT resources, it might be appropriate to charge for services.

Institutional management has to seek out the most advantageous policy for its own institution, and best serve its institutional interests in the competition for funds and resources. At the same time, one can only achieve the necessary infrastructure in the IT domain (network infrastructure and information systems) with combined forces and co-operative pressure in convincing politicians and the public that higher education and research should be the avant-garde in working toward the information society vision.

Financing information technology: the main problem areas

Financing mechanisms -- Co-ordination mechanisms

Financing mechanisms are a means for co-ordinating in and among organisations. This holds for financing IT as well as for other resources and services which form the base of organisations and the interplay among organisations. One can differentiate four general alternatives for financing IT and IT-related services within institutions, as well as for the relationship between institutions and funding governments. These can be thought of as four different co-ordination mechanisms:

Market model

The informational base of the market is price. Those who want to acquire a service or good must pay for it, and before buying they consider price, quality, and the extent to which characteristics of the good or service meet their requirements. These goods or services are supplied only if there is enough demand. For innovative IT technology, which needs to be promoted and can be very expensive in its infant (not yet marketable) stage, the market does not seem to be a suitable model for co-ordinating and financing. In a real market, the customer must have his or her choice of suppliers. If the customer is bound to an inner institutional supplier, one needs rather to talk of "charging" as a co-ordination model more than a market mechanism. The pressure for the supplier to provide outstanding services for reasonable prices is of course higher if they are competing with other suppliers. In the market model, customers are free to purchase a particular good or service, or to spend their money elsewhere. They set their own priorities and time their purchases. The market model applies to both hardware components and most software needed in higher education and research. Many other services such as maintenance, configuration, installation, and counselling, can be contracted out, but only in a few cases have these services been left to the co-ordination of the market mechanism.

Central supply model

IT goods and services are available, regardless of the demands of institutional members, and the scientific community. If IT resources are abundant, no regulations about use are necessary. This model best applies for innovative technology, especially in its early stages when demand may not be overwhelming and restrictions are not necessary. Once the technology is accepted and the number of users significantly increases, three alternatives emerge for funders in the central supply model:

— *Resources are made available according to demand.* This implies that the amount of funds to be top-sliced (*i.e.* not deployed to user-subunits) has to increase accordingly, leaving fewer funds to be allocated at the discretion of the users.

— *Availability of resources is limited.* Then a central system of rules and regulations that determine and limit use will be necessary. In this case, the co-ordination system shows marked bureaucratic traits, and the central supply system turns out to be a central rationing system.

— *Finally, allowing supply to fall behind demand, without restrictions on use* -- the only rule for this co-ordination mechanism is the inconvenience users suffer; it is a rationing system by inconvenience.

It is not difficult to agree that the central supply model applies only to innovative technology in its early pre-marketable stage.

The co-operative model

In this model, participants work together in a club-like style. In co-operation, they agree to put parts of their budgets toward a central supply of resources, and each retains enough influence, on how these central resources are invested, maintained, operated, financed and reinvested. Part of the finances needed for "central" co-operative resources may be recovered through charging users. This helps the user to use resources in a conscious manner and helps central service providers maintain a high level of service. The co-operative model seems best suited to infrastructural IT in its more mature stage, like networks, central information systems, certain software developments, and central computing pools and servers.

The autarky model

In this model, an organisational submit does not allow central, external interference in such things as purchasing, installing, maintaining and operating hardware and software. In their eyes, the model represents a release from the central bureaucracy of the mainframe era. The Autarky model may be of interest to those who already have the expertise, or take a "do-it-yourself" teaching and research approach. Under closer scrutiny, the Autarky model for IT usually turns out to be the least efficient model for the "normal" user, and should be replaced by the co-operative model.

Charging[1]

In two of the models, charging paid a key role. It thus seems worthwhile to focus on some details of charging. Charging in the world of IT seems suitable for mature services where enough demand exists. Charging tends to affect the behaviour of the participants in a system; it affects patterns of use. Charging works effectively as a co-ordination system as it builds on the customer-supplier relationship. Users will place direct pressure on service providers to improve the service, and also become selective and conscious of using the limited resources available. Charging more or less forces costs to become visible.

On the service-providing side, however, one can determine whether to try to recover the total costs of services, or only a certain portion thereof. Another issue is whether all income generated is dedicated to that particular service, or whether older services help finance the development of new ones.

Charging for IT services should be introduced in the following situations:

- there is a largish sum involved;
- the service under review is not experimental, and unrestricted use is encouraged; and
- there is a real need to redistribute funds, to influence patterns of use, or to generate income.

Four models of charging come to mind:

- *Flat-rate charging.* A flat rate is like a membership fee for those who want to use the service. It is the same for all "members" and independent from frequency or volume of use. This kind of charging is closest to top-slicing.

- *Charge proportional to size characteristics.* Size might refer to the number of students, staff, or both of each unit. Or charges might be related to the size of the units budget under review.

- *Charge related to cost.* What cost means in this model of charging depends on whether or not charging should recover full cost of the service. In both cases the user is charged proportionately to his/her use of the service, and to a certain degree the charge reflects the cost, incurred by each user. In reality, it might be very difficult to identify exactly the cost caused by the user, and the fees usually represent only a rough relationship to some quantitative criteria of use.

- *Benefit-related charges.* Here, one tries to assess the different benefits a service represents for a user or user unit, and the service is charged on a proportional basis. It might however be difficult to assess the different benefits of a service for each user.

Charging must be simple, its intended impacts clearly understood, and collection and administration need to be easy to handle.

---

[1] The author is indebted to Mike Tedd, who provided the ideas for this section.

Infrastructure --Innovation

The underlying question for alternative financing models and charging alternatives is whether an IT-related service should be left to decentral user units or the focus of central policy and administration. A systematic review reveals at least two items that should come under central policy, if not top-sliced financing.

The first is innovation. One of the tasks of higher education and research is to develop and promote innovative technology. Often, however, this task exceeds the budget and policy domain of institutional subunits. This is especially the case when the innovation is related to services that should be spread throughout the institution and beyond into the future, before it transcends its innovative stage into a mature (marketable) stage. Innovative technology is usually financed centrally (top-sliced).

The other focus for central institutional policy and provision is IT infrastructure. Infrastructure refers to the widespread existence of computing-front ends, to the network including services on the network. Whether or not infrastructural services are charged or still encouraged, by institutional or governmental incentive and financial programmes, depends on whether a service has entered its mature marketable stage.

Software

Software is increasingly becoming a financial problem as software costs exceed hardware costs. Fortunately, many software categories develop into standard software, meaning that the software pieces, needed by an institution or its subunits, are not unique, but may also be used by many others within the institution and elsewhere. This fact has of course a significant impact on the price of software and allows, on a campus or national level, to negotiate licences with software suppliers. The problem remains however that individual users and user units have to accept standard software as suitable to their work. Another problem is that institutional management and beyond (such as self-organising bodies) have to take the initiative in promoting standard software application and in negotiating special licences.

Software carries another price. There is also a personnel cost incurred when software is installed, configured, when users are trained to maximise its use, and when they have problems and questions. This kind of personnel follow-up cost has to be considered fully when software costs are calculated and software is purchased. In terms of standard software, this kind of personnel support could well be the focus of some central services units.

One category of software for higher education is yet to be very widely developed and used, lacks support and application, and results in duplicated efforts and financial input: software related to teaching (teach-ware, courseware, CBI modules, etc). There are reasons deeply rooted in academic cultures and career patterns that explain this underestimation of teach-ware. One problem is that the act of teaching, and the kind of courses offered, are regarded as individualised and a decision of each scholar. In the case of teach-ware, it is difficult to develop the standards that would have to be accepted. Another impediment is that writing teaching software does not yet fit into reputation and career patterns. The book, the text book or scholar work in printed form, still represents the building block for an academic career and promotion. A third impediment lies in the complexity of handling authoring software for CBI modules. There is, without doubt, a way for institutional management and national research and educational policy to take an active role in the development and exchange of educational software in order to reap the full benefits of efficiency and gains in effectiveness through information technology. Central institutional CBI support units could, for example, place emphasis on helping individual teachers to develop modules or to screen the market and colleagues' activities at other institutions with regards to available software.

Another problem with software is the copyright issue. The more that hardware, system software, and application software become standardised, the easier it is to copy software without purchasing the licences. A higher education institution, however, cannot afford software piracy. This is not an acceptable means to reduce IT-related expenses. It could be a task of central institutional management to provide for campus licences and to organise the central supply of subunits and users with the standard software (software downloading via the campus network from central standard software servers, according to use and according to the number of licences available on campus).

Networking

Networking (local LANs, campus networks, links to national research networks, and the use of international lines, including network services) takes up a large part of IT-related spending. Networking represents the next step in information handling and IT. Not only increased computing power, but also the global multi-media connectivity as well make the difference in the future of information handling. Costs related to network speed and transmission capacity are rising exponentially, and the question remains unsolved as to how institutions can afford to enter the future of information technology. For forward-looking institutions, it is clearly not a solution to state that higher education does not need 34 Mbit or 140 Mbit connectivity. At the low end of speed and transmission capacity, however, it seems feasible to charge users for using the channel, but not without a general budget to allow them to decide on channel use. The question is whether services on the networks, and access to information files, should be subsidised or be free-of-charge to education and research.

Institutional management and managers responsible within the institutions or beyond will have to investigate where integrated use of networks, such as for data and telephone transmission, may help reduce information handling costs. This may depend on national telecommunication price policies beyond the geographic area of the institution.

Information policy

Dealing with information technology and financing information technology does not mean dealing with technology for its own sake. Handling information is the underlying topic, and should be the primary focus of institutional management, when developing IT-related policy and investment plans. More important than the network are network services. The question is what kind of information and information exchange does an institution need, which information should be made available locally, stored and updated, and which kind of information can be purchased or accessed remotely. The virtual electronic library and the virtual global university, including the homes of teachers and learners, is the topic of the future information society and its higher education branch. IT investment policy must always rely on these goals or more modest ones in the same vein.

Financing information technology: summary recommendations for institutional management

This section is meant to summarise the results of discussions from the workshop of experts on IT-related financing, budgeting, and charging problems, to the extent to which they appear in the previous text. The summary will be presented in the form of ten recommendations, without further comment, which will provide reference back to previous sections.

1) Develop and implement an information policy/strategy for the institution, part of which is an IT-investment plan.

2) Try to provide more visibility for the IT-related items in central and decentral budgets and budget-planning processes. Implement a cost tracking system for IT costs.

3) Concentrate the responsibility for information and IT-related issues within the institution, or at least organise strong co-operation among the departments involved.

4) Offer central IT and information services within the institution so as to achieve efficient use of IT resources and to fully exploit the potential of IT (*i.e.* central maintenance services, CBI support units, software licences, and software servers)

5) Charge for central services. Apply charges as an educational tool for users to use services in a conscious way, but do not necessarily expect to recover total costs.

6) Build on the co-operative model of co-ordination and financing.

7) Become involved in the national IT-policy arena in order to promote the pilot role of higher education and research in the future of the information society.

8) Work on the next step in the connectivity for the institution.

9) Invest heavily in the network and information infrastructure of the institution.

10) Provide the latest information technology in at least one place (computer pool) accessible to institution members.

Annex

IT-related indicators for higher education institutions

−   What does an institution spend for IT (estimated percentage of the budget)

−   Computers for students in public pools
    *   typical configuration
    *   number of computers per student
    *   average cost per system (including hardware, software and network connectivity)
    *   reinvestment time

−   Computers for scholars
    *   typical configuration
    *   number of computers per scholar
    *   average cost per system (including hardware, software, and network connectivity)
    *   reinvestment time

−   Central servers
    *   characteristics
    *   proportion of investment sum
    *   reinvestment time

−   Investment in IT for libraries
    *   characteristics
    *   per student/per scholar
    *   reinvestment time

−   Investment in IT for administration and management (centrally and decentrally)
    *   characteristics
    *   per student
    *   reinvestment time

−   Personnel needed per IT unit

−   Campus network (according to characteristics)
    *   investment (related to number of students)
    *   operations cost (related to number of students)
    *   number of front-ends on the network (related to student number and staff number)

−   Cost of connectivity to national research network (9.6 kbit, 64 kbit, 2 Mbit, 34 Mbit, 14 Mbit,...)

- Cost of end-user connectivity to campus network

- Computers owned by students and scholars
  - average characteristics
  - connectivity from home
    - provisions and cost on the owner's side
    - provisions and cost on the institution's side
  - connectivity within the institution
    - provisions and cost on the owner's side
    - provisions and cost on the institution's side

- Charges for IT services within the institution.

Chapter 4

STUDENT-OWNED COMPUTING

by

Gordon Bull
University of Brighton, United Kingdom

Introduction

As the cost of personal computing continues to fall, all the predictions are that more and more students will purchase their own computers. It is expected that this trend will occur across all disciplines although the rate of take-up will vary. There are many problems associated with students owning their own computers if they are to use them productively in their studies other than as stand-alone word processing units. The main issues covered here are:

– the preparation of students for a rapidly changing world;

– improving access to information for staff and students;

– institutional strategies to support student ownership;

– the need for standards;

– the need to base an Information Technology (IT) infrastructure on the institutional goals and missions;

– the central role of the network and the services on the network;

– the need to provide support to enable users to gain maximum benefit from the services provided;

– difficulties associated with changing the culture of an institution; and

– the need to recognise the impact of IT on social as well as academic outcomes.

During the period 1990-1993, the Programme for Institutional Management in Higher Education of the Organisation for Economic Co-operation and Development established a work programme to look in depth at the impact that Information Technology was having on all aspects of higher education. This work programme was carried out by five consultants drawn from five countries and having different views and experiences of higher education. These five consultants visited a number of universities in their own countries to explore in some depth with each the current state and the likely future developments of the use of IT in support of teaching and learning, research, administration, management, and libraries. This work led to a book detailing their findings. Following on from this a number of workshops were held to explore specific topics, one of which was student-owned computing. This paper is based on a synopsis of the findings of that workshop attended by experts from around the world.

Student ownership

It is apparent that the number of students studying at universities who own their own computer is rising. Not only that, but as the cost of personal computing continues to fall, all the predictions are that more and more students will purchase their own computers. It is expected that this trend will occur across all disciplines although the rate of take-up will vary.

There are many problems associated with students owning their own computers if they are to use them productively in their studies other than as stand-alone word processing units. Some of the universities visited as part of the initial study were already responding in a positive way to the potential of student ownership and had established structures and support systems to ensure the maximum benefits for both the students and the university. From the initial findings and from subsequent discussions a number of broad topics were identified as central to the whole debate. These centred around three main issues which might be summarised as academic decisions relating to course design and delivery, resources and how these were provided and controlled, and social aspects to do with culture changes in an institution.

Academic issues

Recent issues of the *Harvard Business Review* suggests that the total knowledge of the world doubles every seven years and that fifty per cent of what many first year university students learn this year will be obsolete by the time they graduate. Students certainly can no longer assume that when they have received their degree or diploma they have finished learning. Given the rate of change it is more important to learn how to learn than it is to master so called facts.

Students need to be prepared for a different world to that of the past. Graduates need to be able to make appropriate, productive and ethical use of the vast sources of information. Few graduates will work in an environment where success is due solely to their own efforts; graduates must be prepared to work with others. To achieve this, students need to be provided with a tool-rich, information-rich environment and to provide a more team-based and project-based learning environment.

Students, tomorrow's problem-solvers, must acquire effective problem-solving strategies, not simply knowledge of the way the world appears to teachers. The solution, easy to state, is to shift the focus of learning from soon obsolete content to flexible techniques by which people can generate new knowledge. Giving students knowledge acquisition strategies is an optimal way to prepare them for ever changing society. IT is an obvious choice for a student's repertoire of learning tools - rapid change generates massive amounts of information, which must be accessed, analysed, reformulated, and communicated in order to derive new knowledge and solutions. A direct implication is that educational goals drastically change. Students have to learn meta-skills, not only for a single course but for all courses - most of the curriculum has to be revised!

Students, teaching staff and support staff will need and want their own computer to avail themselves of the many IT services. As technology continues to become cheaper and better, the price of "end-user devices" will no longer be a barrier for individuals, who will look to their institution to supply an enabling infrastructure. Institutions that do so poorly may be less competitive. The heart of an infrastructure is the network, beginning with the physical medium and continuing through to network service applications, although more than just these technical services must be provided. Network service applications are arrayed along a continuum from content free to content laden. E-mail, a prime example of a productivity tool, is content-free, whilst tools to access scholarly databases, perhaps a network client that accesses the *Oxford English Dictionary,* are content-laden. Support necessary to use the infrastructure advantageously must also be provided, including consulting, training for basic tool use and tool use within the individual's context, such as teaching a mathematical student to create complex formulas in a word-processor, or a language student to efficiently conduct searches of foreign language databases.

The growth of information and in particular the rate at which information becomes obsolete implies that universities need to review their curriculum to take account of this fact. Universities need to ensure that they prepare students for a world in which change is the norm and where they will need to be able to find, understand and interpret new information. This implies that learning to learn is at least as or possibly more important than learning about the current subject material.

As the information age dawns, the need for people who understand the technology has been outstripped by the need for people who understand how information is generated, stored, processed, transmitted, presented, controlled, managed, organised and protected together with the social, economic, political and organisational implications of the information revolution on the information society.

If universities are to survive the pressures on them to educate more students at less cost per student then in addition to using appropriate internal resources, staff and students should look beyond the boundaries of their university to other seats of learning, to other sources of information and to an additional way of working which involves communicating with appropriate people and information sources wherever they may exist in the world. Students and lecturers need services which allow then to get the information they need when they need it. As Rick Spitz of Apple notes "students, lecturers and researchers will need to make contact with others out on the network, collaborating with colleagues or distant experts. Collaborative learning will be critical to learning in the future because much of the information relevant to students is delivered on-line first. If information is doubling every seven years, what is printed on paper becomes obsolete very quickly".

Fundamental to the concept of student-owned computing is the need for the university to provide a range of electronic services to their students (and staff) which adds real value to the ownership of personal computers (and appropriate communication facilities to connect to the campus network). Such an approach, sometimes called the electronic campus, is one of the major costs to the university. It is also something which will require a major culture change within the university if the full benefits are to be achieved.

Institutional strategies to encourage student-owned computing

There is a range of strategies which an institution may adopt in order to facilitate the ownership of or access to personal computing facilities for students. Institutions may choose to reduce the direct cost to a student and hence encourage ownership by a wide range of approaches. Some possible strategies are given below.

Institutions may arrange a loan or a leasing scheme to enable students to meet the cost of purchasing equipment and software. Universities are in an excellent position to ensure that students are able to purchase equipment and software at prices below the commercial market level either through educational discount schemes or by the university purchasing in bulk and passing on the savings to their students. In terms of software this usually means purchasing site licences or purchasing in bulk. Some universities provide the required software free to students, particularly if that software has been generated within the university or by some other body that does not charge for its software. Whatever procedures are adopted they equally apply to software upgrades, which are inevitable.

Some institutions have arranged a buy-back option so that students are able to recover some of the capital cost of their equipment and software at the end of the course. This leaves the university with the problem of what to do with used and often out-of-date technology. Such a policy could be linked to offering students used equipment when they come to the university as an alternative to purchasing new equipment. Such a policy can be made to work where as students progress through their courses they are required to upgrade their systems. In such a situation one approach is for students to sell their starter-level machines to students in earlier years of the course and then purchase the more advanced machine either from students who have completed the course or as a new machine.

An alternative to student-owned computing is the provision of computers by the institution to their students on a loan basis which might well include upgrading them at various points in the course. One reason why a university or department might consider loaning machines to students is to overcome a shortage of space. Each workplace which involves a computer takes around 3m2. The cost of creating sufficient space for a cluster of machines may well exceed the cost of providing a machine for each student who is to use that cluster. Obviously, there are hybrid schemes where costs are shared between university and student in a variety of ways and proportions.

On the communication side there are a number of actions a university can make in order to make ownership more attractive to students. Most universities rely on a mixture of university provided accommodation and private sector accommodation to house their students whilst they are studying (although some countries provide no university accommodation at all). The university can provide links to the campus network to all its own accommodation even to the level of a link for each resident. Such facilities imply that communication costs to the student are zero. For those students who are in non-university accommodation, such a provision is unlikely (although with the introduction of widespread cable TV it may be possible for the university to provide such links at advantageous rates). Where students need to connect to the campus network from non-university locations the usual solution is to make use of the public telephone system using modems. There are three basic costs associated with this form of communication. There is a capital cost associated with the purchase of a modem attached to the student's computer (there is also a requirement for the university to provide modems at the network end), there is the cost of installation and subsequent rental of a phone line, and there is the cost of making calls on the phone line to make connection to the campus network. The university can address such costs in a variety of ways.

One of the costs faced by students with their own computers is that of printing. Universities can chose to recover the costs associated with this in a variety of ways or indeed to not pass on such costs to their students in a direct way. If students are encouraged or obliged to purchase printers then the financial arrangements that can be made to assist such purchases are as discussed above. In terms of the direct cost of printing such as paper and ribbons or cartridges the university may provide these items freely within the teaching accommodation and/or the residential accommodation. It may chose to offer free printing for low quality output using such devices as dot-matrix printers or line-printers but charge for quality output such as from laser printers.

Many universities have internal maintenance and repair facilities for personal computers. In such circumstances it would be possible to offer free or subsidised maintenance and repair services to students. Where the university uses external services it may be in a position to negotiate a better price from such suppliers on the basis of a greater volume of activity for the external company to the advantage of both the students and the university.

Social issues

Human and social aspects are products not only of technical but also of organisational, educational and environmental interactions including information, communication and reward systems.

There are a range of groups within a university who will be affected by a widespread ownership of computers, including students, academic staff, administrative staff, technical staff and the management of the university. The impact on these various group will vary. Some of the outcomes may be quite acceptable, whilst others could be considered poor.

There will be an impact on academic and support staff at all levels which will involve the need for training and for staff to accept new, flexible work practices. Producing an "electronic university" will have a major impact on how the institution works. Though there are costs, this new electronic environment has many potential savings to offer in terms of efficiency across the entire institution including administrative processes, research activities and teaching and learning.

The main benefits of students having ready access to computers are to do with increasing the openness of learning, giving students the ability to exercise more choice with regard to where they study, how they study, when they study and what they study. Part of this is to do with giving students access to the rapidly growing world of electronic information and the interactive nature of much of this. In particular, the ability of students to seek information, store it, process it, reformat it, and to incorporate it into their own work.

Part of it is to do with making the students more completely IT literate and to enable them to communicate with their peers, their teachers and the general community of world-wide scholars and to participate in ongoing discussions on electronic bulletin boards. Part of it is to do with the creation of their own Personal Data Archive (PDA) as a personal view of the discipline they are studying. Such a PDA can form the basis of a lifelong PDA which can grow and develop throughout their life. Part of it is to do with the ability for students to make use of the computer as a modelling tool to explore issues which would otherwise be impossible or impractical. Such simulations can be of benefit in many disciplines across the social and natural sciences, in engineering and technology and in the arts.

Conclusions

Implicit in the above is a new paradigm of learning. The student needs to be able to make sense of an ever increasing information base and to use a wide range of network services to inter-relate with peers, tutors and others in new ways. The emphasis in this meta-learning paradigm is on information not on technology. The stand alone micro computer used for word processing and little else is not the appropriate paradigm. Students must learn to make use of network services in the way they make use of a phone (i.e. they must not regard it as a barrier rather as a natural communication channel). Failure to recognise this can lead to rejection of IT by non-specialists.

In considering the benefits one must recognise that the first order consequences of a technology are relatively easy to predict whereas the second and third order consequences as the technology becomes pervasive are less obvious yet potentially more far reaching. Institutions need to recognise that some consequences will be surprises, so any attempt fully to control and contain costs or predict the social changes will inevitably be fruitless; some provision must be made for contingencies, and the funding arrangements must be flexible.

Many of the effects of student-owned computing will impact a university with or without a policy on the matter. More and more students will unilaterally acquire computers and in doing so exert a range of pressures on the institution. In particular there will be strong pressure to provide these students with more and more electronic services. There are substantial benefits for the institutions to support or encourage such a move so long as the process is well managed and conscious, rather than haphazard or accidental. Those who do not plan for student-owned computing and do not issue guidelines to their students will be unable to cope with the plethora of equipment and software which students will have. Such a situation will lead to frustration by the students and an inability to cope with the demands by the institution.

Institutions will need to fully explore the wide ranging financial and social implications of moving towards an electronic campus before making any decisions. Institutions will need to decide how much of the cost of student ownership to take on themselves, or to try to ameliorate. In particular, consideration of the effect that "recommended" ownership might have on disadvantaged groups. The range of information services an institution will provide will of course depend on many factors within the institution.

For an institution to consider how to provide an optimal information infrastructure it should consider its goals and missions, the roles that IT might provide, the support services needed to use IT in the service of goals and missions, as well as the start-up and ongoing costs, including opportunity costs. An IT infrastructure does not exist for its own sake, but is derived from and constructed to support and in some cases, enable, the academic mission of the institution. Within an institution's consideration of IT, the option of encouraging or requiring all students to have a computer should also be considered. It could be argued that it is more desirable to create an IT infrastructure than for all students to have a computer, although all students having a computer, whilst perhaps an economic luxury, can be seen as a benefit to an institution's academic mission. Moreover, in the near future it is likely that more and more students will either arrive with their own computers or acquire them during their studies.

The way in which an institution sets about developing new courses, new delivery mechanisms and courseware to support the courses will depend on a number of factors. Without suitable incentives to staff to make the kind of changes outlined above, such development will not be sustained. Study leave time to prepare material, reduced teaching and administrative loads, recognition of this activity as a factor contributing to promotion and the provision of adequate supporting resources are all ways of encouraging and sustaining such an activity. Institutions need to recognise the size of the investment required, and how little of it is hardware (the only visible part). The introduction of new teaching and learning processes, the training of staff and students alike in the use of the new technology and the general change in the culture required of an institution are all time consuming and expensive.

REFERENCES

Bull, G.M. *et al.* (1994), *Information Technology -- Issues for Higher Education Management,* Higher Education Policy Series No 26, Jessica Kingsley Publishers, London.

Spitz, R. (1995), *Higher Education News,* Vol. 1, No. 2, Apple Computer Inc., February.

Chapter 5

EXECUTIVE INFORMATION SYSTEMS FOR INSTITUTIONAL MANAGEMENT IN HIGHER EDUCATION

by

Edgar Frackmann

EIS: a new management fad?

In both industry and in higher education, Executive Information Systems (EIS) have emerged as an information technology topic for top-management. But, this is not the whole truth. Information technology can never be an aim in itself. Information technology concerns the processing of information. Only if information processing for top-management and by top-management becomes more important will the importance of information technology for managerial support increase equally.

In industry and commerce, information is becoming an ever more strategic factor in terms of an organisation's competitiveness and survival, and the use of information technology has moved closer to companies' strategic goals. What is being offered under the label of EIS is being developed, discussed, and implemented in industry in the same phase when information technology in general is gaining strategic relevance for corporate world organisations.

Admittedly, higher education has its own laws, rules, cycles and management fads. Nonetheless, there are clear signs that higher education institutions are facing certain challenges where institutional managers are highly likely to follow the example of their corporate colleagues in looking for more efficient and effective information supplies in the context of their managerial activities. This will prompt them to investigate Executive Information Systems.

Executive information in the context of information management

Dealing with EIS means dealing with *information* for top-management, whether in industry or higher education. The following are the main questions that are to be raised in this context:

– Do institutional managers deal more or less systematically with information in the context of their managerial tasks? What kind of information and information support do institutional managers need?

- Where do they get this information from? What are the sources for management information? How is this information being handled by the suppliers, and managers themselves? How is the information supply to be organised most efficiently and effectively?

- What is the possible role of information technology in terms of managerial information requirements and information support? Which aspects are EIS meant to take over in this context?

Information for management is to be seen and organised in the context of overall institutional information management, informational infrastructure, and information logistics.

In higher education, information is dealt with in various contexts. As an information- intensive industry, the primary use of information and information processing is in its primary processes: teaching, learning, and research, *i.e.* in the course of knowledge generation, spread, and transfer. This is not however the topic of this paper.

In higher education, information is dealt with in managerial contexts. Three purposes of managerial information can be identified which should be generated, used, and mediated in higher education:

- information for internal and external reporting and accountability purposes (including president's report, data delivery to statutory bodies, strategic plans, public relations);

- information for marketing purposes (including fund-raising, budgeting negotiations, attracting students, attracting researchers, positioning the institution in its environment); and

- information for problem identification and problem-solving.

Higher education institutions are characterised by very "flat" organisational structures of only "loosely coupled" organisational subunits. There is no concentration of decision- making power. Decisions are made in a network of more informal links, where "centres" of decision-making are difficult to identify.

However, external pressure and surrounding circumstances tend to force an institution as a whole or department to develop, maintain, and implement organisational strategies. It thus follows that the systematic processing of information in higher education institutions is induced more "extrinsically" than "intrinsically". Governments and other statutory bodies request information for accountability purposes, the concerned public deals with such "hot issues" as length of studies, drop-out and attrition rates, the role of higher education in the national economy, quality, and financing higher education. External factors are the primary forces behind involvement with information concerning the institution itself and its functioning within the social and economic environment, *i.e.* management information:

- certain tendencies are visible within the public higher education sector toward granting institutions more institutional autonomy; thus it is to be expected that more of the decisions made so far on the level of government will shift to institutions;

- tightening public purses are moving institutions into more market-like situations, where they have to convince their customers of their competitive advantages; and

- governments and a critical public are no longer content to have input-oriented information, but ask institutions to provide them with more evidence of their performances and output.

Under these new circumstances, information cannot just be "administered" by clerks and generated for statutory bodies without the involvement of institutional management. Information becomes a crucial ingredient of managerial activity. The administrative context of information processing needs to be transcended in a movement towards management information. Management information is used more than once a year to produce presidential reports; consequently the question arises how the generation and processing of information can be made more efficient and effective.

One may contend that an institution's self-generation of information could make it more vulnerable to external steering. Indeed, information about institutional performances (strengths as well as weaknesses) enhances the steering capacity of governments and customers in a market for higher education services. There is however no alternative to generating and working with management information, because to refrain from management information also means to weaken institutional self-regulation capacities, and thus to increase further an institution's vulnerability.

"Information is the key linking element in the different work the manager does" (Mintzberg, 1973). There are three different ways, in which managers deal with information:

- Managers *receive information* actively or passively. They have to monitor the internal and external environment of the institution or organisational unit in order to understand and react to strengths and weaknesses of their institutions, opportunities, and outside threats.

- Managers have to *communicate* within the institution and with outsiders.

- Managers make decisions. Here they need not only information about the actual and planned status, differences between them, and problems to be solved. They also need to communicate with their peers and subordinates in the course of decision-making. Finally, they can *use models* of reality in a more or less conscious manner. While managers may well have their "mental model" of reality, they might be ready and willing to confront their "inner model" with external models. These models might either serve to document, communicate, evaluate, or analyse reality, to test, simulate, forecast, and answer what-if questions regarding problems to be solved, or they might even offer solutions or optimise available resources."

These three categories of information handling have their equivalent in terms of potential information technology support. *Information supply, communication support,* and *modelling support* can be distinguished as possible features of information and communication technology, which need to be embedded in overall institutional information management, or those management activities which guarantee that the right information is:

- available;
- at the right time;
- in the right place; and
- with the "right" costs.

Information management also means to identify the strategic benefits of both information handling, and information and communication technology investments for the sake of organisational survival. Using information and communication technology for institutional management cannot be an isolated undertaking, but has to be organised in the context of information management and institutional information and communication support.

To conceptualise and construct management information support in higher education institutions is no easy endeavour, since it is difficult to identify "centres" of higher education decision-making. Apart from those government decisions highly relevant to each institution, it is necessary at the very least to differentiate, among the board or council, president or executive team, secretary general and administration, collegiate bodies such as the senate and department council, deans, institutes and chairholders, and finally all "hidden leaders and decision makers". Even if the institution is regarded as hierarchically organised with a top chief decision-maker for a department or institution as a whole, this does not imply top-down decision-making processes. More than in other organisations, in professional organisations like the university, decisions are made bottom-up, strategies emerge rather than be set, decisions need intensive communication and legitimisation, and there are authorisation processes.

As a consequence, information support in higher education institutions, cannot be conceived as just delivering information to an individual decision-maker at the top of an organisational unit or institution as a whole. More than in other organisations, information support in higher education means:

- sharing information support;
- providing the subunit or institution with an "organisational memory";
- providing communication support; and
- providing group decision support and decision process support (workflow management).

But even if information support and information technology support in higher education are seen rather as serving a group, subunit, or organisation as a whole, at the "end of the line" at the computer terminal -- the individual manager, decision-maker, or simply a member of the organisation are those processing information, the end-users, with or without computer support.

Three categories of end-users of computerised information and communication support can be distinguished (cf. Rockart and Flannery, 1983):

- the *indirect end-user* uses the computer through other people and benefits only indirectly from information systems and computer support;

- the *intermediate end-user* specifies the information requirements for reports he/she ultimately receives, but does not use the computer system "hands-on"; and

- the *direct end-users* actually use computer terminals themselves and process information themselves with the aid of information and communication systems.

Moving from these preliminary remarks on information processing, information support and computer systems in higher education institutions, it is now appropriate to investigate the EIS for institutional management in higher education in more detail.

What institutional managers should know about EIS

Some definitions

The term Executive Information System first came into broader use at the end of the 1980s for commercial software products that provided a desk-top "front-end" for managers to select and present computerised information. However, one of the first definitions of EIS dates back to the early 1980s: an EIS should be "oriented towards assembling the necessary relevant planning and control data in an information data base, providing the desired access mechanisms, and establishing the relevant organisational support mechanisms to assist the users" (Rockart and Treacy, 1980).

More recently, Thierauf wrote, "An executive information system consists of newer computer technology, including data sources and programs that locate the data desired, place it in common format, massage it into useful form, and present it as useful information for the executive (...). An executive information system can be defined in its broadest sense as one that deals with all of the information that helps an executive make strategic and competitive decisions, keeps track of the overall business and its functional units, and cuts down on the time spent on routine tasks performed by an executive. As such, an EIS is capable of providing an executive with the right information in the right format, fast enough to enable the individual to make the right decision" (Thierauf, 1991).

According to these definitions, the efforts of software producers, and the wording of the term EIS, the main emphasis of Executive Information Systems is directed to the following areas:

– information support;
– for top-management (executives); and
– through computer systems.

Some remarks about the history of computer support for management

Without knowledge of the history of computer support for management and top-management, it would be difficult to understand the new emphasis and the new thrust of EIS. The history of computer support for management -- more a history of failures than a success story -- can be seen in three phases each with its own "tags":

– the Management Information System (MIS) phase;
– the Decision Support System (DSS) phase; and
– the Executive Information System (EIS) phase.

Management Information Systems (MIS)

In the early 1970s, the "total systems approach" meant that whatever information system was developed and implemented within the organisation, it was to serve top-management. Information requirements were to be derived top-down from what top-management was thought to need. In reality, Management Information Systems turned out to represent the penetration of data processing systems throughout the company (in higher education, the administrative computing systems). Management Information Systems served mass-data processing, and their main goal was to *automate*. MIS focused on managing mass information rather than information supply for management. Any information delivered in computerised form to management consisted of piles of computer printouts, which contributed to a significant reluctance of managers towards computer support in general. Management Information Systems represented the era of automation, and had very little to do with computer support for managers.

Decision Support Systems (DSS)

At the end of the 1970s and early 1980s, a new approach to support management with computer systems was launched with the name Decision Support System. Here the idea was to support management by approaching activities which represent managerial foci more typically than unspecified information handling. Decisions are identified as the most crucial part of managers' work, and hence to be supported by the then state-of-the-art computer systems. Not just information supply, but more sophisticated analytical tools were to be the main focus of DSS. Models and modelling support turned out to be the new conceptual approach of DSS. In one of the most important books on DSS at that time, they were defined (Keen/Scott Morton 1978) in the following way:

> "Decision Support Systems (DSS) represent a point of view on the role of the computer in the management decision making process. Decision support implies the use of computers to:
>
> — assist managers in their decision process in semi-structured tasks;
> — support, rather than replace managerial judgement; and
> — improve the effectiveness of decision making rather than its efficiency."

In practice, however, it turned out that top-management did not seek computer support in a very sophisticated manner. "For many top level line managers...the concept of decision support fails to equate very well with the way they view their jobs. Decision support is, in effect, a middle management concept. The decisions top executives make, however, are non-repetitive, ever-changing and moment-to-moment. There is no time to build a system for each of their decisions. The DSS orientation is therefore inadequate and even misleading in the conceptualisation of top managerial use of computer-based information" (Rockart and Treacy, 1980).

DSS represent the era in which information technology transcended mere automation as a tool to support, and not simply to replace human tasks. For the first time in the history of information technology, DSS represent the concept of information support rather than conceiving and implementing information technology to replace human beings in the labour process.

Executive Information Systems (EIS)

EIS represent the software industry answer to deficiencies of prior attempts to support managers with information technology. Executive Information Systems are conceived as highly user-friendly front-ends, as close as possible at the individual manager, whether a direct end-user or intermediate end-user.

EIS can be seen as a revival of the MIS idea in that the main emphasis is on *information supply* for chief executives. The approach, however, is not to deliver information per se, nor as much information as possible, but rather to select, filter, or add information on request, and to provide easy and quickly comprehensible information (graphical presentation among other modes). With the emphasis on information, EIS also addresses a failure of sophisticated analytical tools for top-managers. But even those managers who feel more computer literate, and see systematic use of information as a crucial ingredient of their work, can use such additional EIS features as trend extrapolation and what-if-analysis. Considering that a high proportion of a manager's working day is spent on communication processes, an EIS usually provides electronic-mail and other communication support features incorporated in the computer user-interface. With these extensions, an EIS could also be called an *Executive Support System* (Rockart and DeLong, 1988).

Managers' systematic reasons for not applying computer systems support

The history of computer support for managers is no success story. There are two categories of systematic impediments to supporting managers with computer systems. One refers to a systematic, planned, active use of information, the other to interaction with a computer system, *i.e.* problems of user-interface and physical access to computerised information. Only if EIS and computer systems, with whatever name tag, are able to cope with these systematic impediments can they really assist managers in their daily information handling tasks. The failures of computer support so far may thus be useful to help define the requirements EIS will have to meet in order to be accepted by managers.

Brevity, fragmentation, and variety of managerial work

The manager's working day is characterised by extreme fragmentation, a sequence of short and diverse activities. Managers do not have time to sit back, contemplate, and complete lengthy analytical work at the screen and computer keyboard. They can neither afford extended set-up times for each activity, nor to "fight" with complex access and handling mechanisms to get the information they need. Computer systems accessed only via extensive training and user manuals, and where information is not immediately comprehensible, is unacceptable to managers.

"Desk work" versus "outside office activities"

Empirical investigations show that managers spend only a small proportion of time at their desks (cf. Mintzberg, 1973: 22 per cent). This implies that managers can be only non-frequent users of their computerised information systems, unless these systems become "mobile," and that managers cannot waste their time with user access problems.

Communication

Empirical investigations also demonstrate what every manager might confirm: managerial activities consist of communication (meetings, phone calls, tours, etc.) more than any other mode of information processing. Any considerable gain in efficiency to be achieved through computer support must also focus to a certain extent on communication support.

Verbal, informal, and visual communication based information

Much of the information received and handled by managers, is verbal and visual, and is transmitted in the context of informal communication. A computerised information support for managers that focuses only on quantitative (numerical) information is of limited value to managers.

Information "overload"

Managers do not suffer from a lack of information, but rather from an information overload. The MIS failure was mainly due to lack of selection mechanisms, and the low quality of information supply in terms of the user-friendliness of user-interface.

External information

The higher a manager's position in the hierarchical ladder of an organisation, the more he or she will have to rely on external information as opposed to information accrued within the organisation. If an information system provides only "internal" information, its usefulness will be limited for this category of managers.

"Satisfying" view of decision-making

In their decision-making processes, managers do not follow the "rational model" of decision-making, where they would continue to seek information until they have total information and can make an optimal choice. With strategies for reducing complexity, they instead limit the amount of information to be considered, and they seem to be very successful with "satisfying" instead of "maximising" problem-solving techniques. The role of a computer system can thus not simply be to expand the amount of information considered by the decision maker since this would only increase complexity.

No extensive analytical work with information

Due to restrictions on their time, managers do not sit back and intensively use analytical tools. In terms of analysis, they instead rely on support staff after generating and communicating some more or less fuzzy ideas. The main emphasis of computerised information system support thus seems to fall rather on information delivery to managers, and that in a form in which exceptions and deviations from standard values can be captured very quickly.

Non-routine, non-repetitive problems to be solved

Managers have to deal with non-routine, non-repetitive problems. Other problems can easily be handled by subordinates or even by computer systems. If computer systems are to assist managers in solving "unique" problems, they must be able to point to exceptional situations, and they cannot always deliver the same set of information. The EIS has to be fed with ever-changing information domains.

Keyboard and computer using problems

Many managers do not like using keyboards or secretary-typing and therefore do not like computer support where they are direct end-users. Only if physical access to the computerised information relies as little as possible on keyboard input will managers be candidates for direct computer use.

Decision-making in higher education institutions

In higher education institutions, one might well ask whether there is indeed a need for information in decision making. One might consider that the most important decisions are made on governmental levels instead of within institutions. Or one might have difficulties seeing where within institutions deliberate decision making takes place with the systematic use of information in the decision-making processes. Only with clear-cut responsibilities beyond the commitment of individual teachers and researchers to the teaching and research processes, increasing institutional autonomy, and organised decision making within the institution, can there be a relevant need for systematic information supply.

What EIS offer

In order to be useful and well-accepted tools for institutional managers, Executive Information Systems have to possess certain characteristics and provide certain support features. The revival of the idea of managerial computer support should not be nurtured only by a new generation of more computer-literate managers with a sophisticated understanding of information, but rather by mature technologies to assist managers in their "eternal" information and information-processing needs. Executive Information Systems should provide a solution to manager's main information-handling problems.

Problem of limited time

With an EIS, a manager does not need to waste time in order to identify relevant information among a plethora of items. Information is presented in a pre-selected manner, according to those critical factors of success the manager wants to monitor regularly. The EIS provides features to report exceptions, such as colour coding techniques. In case the manager wants to go into more detail, to search for sources of the exceptions, the system provides drill-down facilities. The response time for seeking information files is very short. This is due to the implementation of EIS on a PC (MS-WINDOWS or PS/2 or MacIntosh).

Problems using computers

The EIS has self-explanatory capacities. Everything the user has to do in order to access desired information is explained in a graphical mode, and almost all of the input is possible through a mouse instead of keyboard. A future generation of EIS will even provide voice input.

Actuality

An EIS cannot survive in its managerial environment unless it provides information with a high degree of actuality. The PC-based EIS is only the front-end for information retrieval. An immediate information up-date can be guaranteed only if the PC has a host computer connection, from which internal and external information is downloaded as soon as data change over time.

Trigger-information

Managers do not just "consume" information by itself. The most important information is that which induces immediate activity or triggers follow-up actions. The EIS thus has to provide the manager with a functionality in order, for example, to send information received to subordinates, add annotations to the information, or use recall-facilities in order to retrieve this information in due course or under certain conditions.

Communication

Receiving information has to be coupled with sending information as a functionality of an EIS. Since managers spend the biggest proportion of their own time on communications, EIS have to facilitate communication as well.

External information

Managers do not only monitor information generated by their own organisation, but also external information, comparative data on other institutions, demographic data, or economic data. The Executive Information System has to provide external information to the manager. The EIS can either be linked to external computerised sources of information such as private or public information services, or be updated by feeding CD-ROMs containing external information with longer renewal cycles into the system on a regular basis.

Non-quantitative, non-structured information

According to managers' information requirements, EIS not only provide numerical, quantitative data, but also text and business graphics. The next generation of systems will also provide multi-media information such as images, video, and voice.

Individuality

An EIS has to take into account that managers are different individuals. What kind of information is provided by an EIS depends on what the individual manager/user regards as critical for the success and survival of the organisation under his or her responsibility. In terms of its access modes, an EIS also has to distinguish whether the manager is a frequent or non-frequent user, and whether the user is a novice or advanced user.

Mobility

Because a manager spends only a limited time at the desk, the EIS has to cope with mobility. Notebooks containing relevant information and capable of plugging into information channels from home or while travelling are the adequate technological answers to managers' information handling needs.

Why do institutional managers need Executive Information Systems now?

As in industry, there is a certain "pressure" from providers of EIS-software to implement and use Executive Information Systems. Since the software exists that can present information in a manager-like manner (easy to handle), information managers would need with or without IT-support, why not convince managers that they should have such a system on their desks, in their homes, in trains and planes, and in their hotel rooms while travelling?

However, this "technology push" would have no impact without other "pressure" towards a more intensive or more efficient use of information. In higher education, there is increasing institutional autonomy and exposure to market-like situations and accountability pressure. Given these circumstances, institutions as organisations, along with their managers and those involved in decision-making, are increasingly forced to generate and use information about the organisation and its environment more consciously and deliberately. Information handling becomes a formal, structured endeavour beyond informal communication channels. Gathering and spreading information becomes more time consuming, given the amount of information to be considered and the number of communication partners involved. This increasing need to process information is challenging institutions just at the time when efficiency and cost containment are the agenda. With greater autonomy, institutions cannot simply request more funds from the public purse, because information became more expensive. Information and communication have become a relevant cost factor within the organisational setting of a higher education institution.

In this situation, where there is concurrently a greater need for information, and communication and improved efficiency, it is important to note that information is already available in computerised form (administrative computing systems, external information files) and need not be entered, in order to be transferred and presented. Moreover, electronic communication channels (campus network, regional, national, and international research networks) exist, providing the infrastructure with rapid and efficient transfer of information to where it is needed.

Whatever information is needed in whatever managerial activities within institutional settings, one should thus first investigate whether this information can be made available without interference that consumes human time, and without paper printouts to be re-entered into computer systems in order to transfer, present or otherwise process the information.

What does information support mean?

While Executive Information Systems are meant to provide managerial information support, they cannot provide everything to everybody. They have certain strengths and priorities in their services; one should expect only what they are able to provide. In this light, it thus seems useful to consider the use of managerial information in higher education settings in order to identify what EIS can and should support.

The context of information use

As mentioned earlier, three contexts of managerial information use in higher education institutions can be identified:

- information for reporting and accountability purposes;
- information for marketing purposes; and
- information in the context of problem identification and problem solving.

The most suitable information items to include in Executive Information Systems and to present to managers through Executive Information Systems are those to be used in all three contexts. For example, drop-out rates can be used in departmental and presidential reports, reports to external statutory bodies, to convince students to enrol in a particular programme at an institution, or to help monitor problems related to attrition/retention. Efficiency demands that information needed in multiple contexts should not be filed, updated, and entered into electronic form more than once.

The main emphasis of EIS is on status information and information presentation, not on providing problem-solving models. EIS facilitates monitoring, early warning, exception reporting, and threshold value reporting. Once the information is stored, it can be presented in reports, whether printed or transferred electronically to whomever the information concerns. In terms of information support for decision-making, one can distinguish several information categories:

- information about planned, expected values;
- information about differences between actual and expected/planned values;
- status information before decision implementation, as compared with status information after decision implementation; and
- a repertoire of possible problem-solving alternatives.

The priority of EIS is on the first three categories. Problem- solving models or analytical tools are also very useful in higher education settings, such as models for forecasting enrolment, resource planning, and resource allocation. They are however more useful in the hands of support staff and functional managers in higher education institutions than for general managers. The main emphasis of EIS is on monitoring rather than on analysis support.

Input, process, and output-information

Higher education can be seen as "production or service delivery processes" in which certain input variables are used in a "production process" to deliver an output. These processes take place within an internal and an external environment. Here information is generated and processed that concerns institutional management. Figure 5.1 depicts this context of managerial information in higher education institutions.

In terms of external information requests, a tendency is emerging to shift from input- oriented to output-related information. While government and the public appeared content thus far with knowing that resources devoted to higher education were used properly and according to public accounting rules, one hears more and more often doubts about the quality of higher education, and if the public receives appropriate return on money invested in higher education. As mentioned earlier, the shift in required information induces institutional management to get involved in generating and spreading information, making the delivery of information to external bodies a management activity rather than one for clerks and accounting systems. While input data could rely heavily on administrative computing systems (such as accounting system, personnel administration and payroll system, physical plant, and student records system), output data, especially if qualitative data are required, have to rely on more sophisticated and expensive sources, such as regular surveys, peer reviews, and external comparative data, in order to position the institution within its competitive environment. The following list provides some examples of information categories from these broader domains: input, output, process, and internal and external environments (Figure 5.2).

Ad hoc *versus reusable information*

One can differentiate between decisions which rely on continuously monitored and regularly updated information, where problems are identified through deviations from standard values (exception reporting), and decisions which have to rely on information totally unknown to date, where the situation is unique.

Executive Information Systems can provide immediate assistance for the first category of decision-making and information requirements. They have limitations, however, in the latter category of decisions and information requirements. At the same time, an EIS well-embedded in a staff support infrastructure may easily be extended to provide information not included in EIS services thus far. Indeed, an EIS never should stick to a set structure and information domain. Information requirements can change over time, and individual EIS users may also find their information needs modified in the course of using the system and making decisions. That is the reason why an EIS has to be maintained by staff members who form an *Executive Information Service*.

The question may however emerge as to how fast information domains change over time in higher education, and how fast decisions that depend on *ad hoc* information are to be made in higher education. Higher education is an endeavour whose impacts are long-lasting, production processes are rather long compared with many industries, innovation rates in organisational processes are slower, and decisions tend to follow a semester cycle rather than a monthly cycle. In industry, some fixed indicators change very rapidly, and those responsible for the organisation under review might be interested to know the actual figures of ROI, profit, or turn-over rate, at least on a monthly basis, if not more frequently.

In higher education, it is striking that facts do not change as rapidly as in industry; still it seems far more difficult to identify or build a consensus around indicators that provide information about the performance of higher education institutions. This array of indicators can change more frequently than in industry according to what politicians, the public, or customers contend as important. Thus such considerations as efficiency, length of studies, quality of teaching and educational outcomes, and attrition and retention rates, are left not only to individual institutional managers. Again, an EIS is forged by the manager/user as well as by external forces and their pressure on higher education.

Information on the past versus information on the future

An EIS cannot conceive the future, nor can it provide the managers with future visions for the higher education institution or each sub-unit. The main emphasis of an EIS is to provide the manager with information, information that is available as soon as "things have happened". An EIS is not a decision support system, where its primary purpose would cover forecasting models, trend extrapolation, what-if analysis, or simulations. This could be an addendum to providing information to those managers who wish to do analytical work with information on the past. The average direct end-user manager, however, will not use the keyboard and screen to do analytical work. With or without an EIS, a manager's judgement and visions will still largely determine the strategic decisions for each organisation. Goals attached to an EIS should not be too ambitious since this can impede, rather than promote, any benefits that may be drawn from an EIS.

Internal versus external information

Internal information is admittedly the best available information to feed into an EIS. All administrative computing files can provide valuable information for the EIS. Other information otherwise entered into machine-readable form for producing presidential reports and other public relations material and statutory reports is also useful. Systematically reviewing all internal gathering, storing, and presentation of information will not only lead to an efficient nurturing of the EIS, but will also improve efficiency and avoid redundancy in overall information processing within the institutional realm.

Internal information can, however, develop its full potential only if it is put into the context of external information. Managers and decision-makers need comparable information about other institutions and comparable sub-units, such as national data on students, staff, finances, and research projects. Many of these regional and national data are available in machine-readable form or may easily be entered as such by scanning. Once EIS use is widespread in the higher education scene, institutions can form alliances to exchange comparable data they need to position their own data in the context of peer institutions and sub-units.

Structured, quantitative versus verbal and unstructured information

The information generated in administrative computing systems, and that can be downloaded to the EIS is quantitative information on students, exams, finances, staff, space, or equipment. Indeed, this kind of quantitative information is very important for institutional managers to monitor closely the course of institutional activities. This quantitative data should not only be presented as figures, but also in the form of charts and graphs. The main advantage and benefit of using an EIS is that managers can learn to look at information in a more visual way, first graphs and colours indicating "exceptions" and then details with exact figures and sources of deviations. The EIS allows one to move easily among modes of presentation.

Many other kinds of information exist that are not numerical and quantitative, including texts of laws, regulations, prior decisions, memos and messages, addresses, and organisational charts, along with descriptions of research projects, programs, and admission standards. An EIS should not be limited to presenting quantitative data in tables and graphs, but should also include texts and charts, as deemed useful by the manager/user.

Management indicators

Executive Information Systems should provide management indicators -- a claim more easily said than done. Management indicators are often referred to as "Critical Success Factors". According to Bullen and Rockart, "Critical Success Factors (CSFs) are the limited number of areas in which satisfactory results will ensure successful competitive performance for the individual, department, or organisation. CSFs are the few key areas where `things must go right' for the business to flourish and for the manager's goals to be attained" (Bullen and Rockart, 1986, p. 385).

In both the definition and as mentioned earlier, management indicators or critical success factors have partially to do with organisation's ability to survive and compete within its environment, and partially with each manager's perception of this strategic scene, as well as his or her goals in this respect. These last determinants are very difficult to define and identify, and rely heavily on the manager's willingness to receive support from an EIS.

Management indicators are linked to the performance of a higher education institution, and provide information about the tasks of an institution or its presumed responsibilities within its environment. Management indicators have something to do with the interface between the institution and its environment, that is its input or intake, as well as its output, quality, and performances. Management indicators are oriented to decision-making and problem-solving. Information is provided not only for its own sake, but to monitor areas where problems may emerge and alternative solutions are to be sought in order to cope with these issues seen as crucial for the institution or sub-unit. Some managers may, for example, choose to monitor the following questions:

− How do we perform in terms of the length of studies in our programmes in comparison with other institutions?

− What are the relevant figures for drop-out and attrition?

− What do we know about our graduates on the labour market?

− What do we spend on one student from the first to last day of his/her educational career at our institution?

− What do we spend on our administration?

− What proportion of our overall funds is devoted to library services, information services, information and communication technology, etc.?

− What do we know about the "productivity" of our staff members (publications, research projects, teaching load, number of graduates)?

− What proportion of our budget is spent on salaries in each department?

Extending the supporting services of an EIS: the Executive Support System

The most important feature of an EIS is to provide institutional managers with *information*. This is the primary emphasis of an EIS, and one should not start to overload an EIS with a plethora of functions, complex functional menus through which a user must navigate to reach the tiny bit of functionality needed on a regular basis.

Only more advanced users, more frequent users, and computer-literate and sophisticated managers may want to spend more time at the computer and accomplish more, once they handle information in a computer-supported fashion. Then the EIS needs to provide a set not of simply additional, but integrated services. Here it is important not only for switching among services to be possible, but that information be transferred from one information-related service to another, to avoid intermediate printout and data re-entry, to provide memory aid, and to secure an easy information transfer from the manager's mind and working place to others within and outside the organisation. It is thus vital that integrated services are offered to the user under the "umbrella" of an integrated graphical user interface, with easily comprehensible graphic symbols for the available functions, and the switching and navigating facilities necessary to seek, process and transfer information. In addition to the information supply function, available facilities under the "umbrella" of an EIS user interface might include the following.

Communication

Communication facilities, such as e-mail (message handling), could be a service for institutional members that even precedes core EIS functions (information supply). Some institutional managers may want to plug into institutional informal and semi-formal communication channels before they are served with the more formal and structured information services provided by an EIS.

Once the manager has access to an EIS, able to deliver information, he or she may want to send selected EIS templates with questions and remarks to subordinates and colleagues, ask questions about the information delivered, or send to-do-lists based on EIS information. Communication services need thus to be linked directly to the core EIS information provision, so that, for example, on-screen information can be transferred with textual and other add-ons.

Personal files

The manager not only wants to transfer information received through the EIS or electronic mail, but to store and recall it at a later date or according to certain events or dates as well. He or she might also choose to keep personal memos and other information received electronically or otherwise.

Word processing

Some managers are computer literate enough to type their own texts instead of dictating. Word processing facilities can be incorporated into the integrated services of an EIS. In this case, the text exchange facilities with the manager's secretary are essential to putting the finishing touches and mailing them off on whatever channels.

Fax

Fax has developed into the most convenient, fast, and inexpensive means of communication, and most information recipients are accessible via fax. Managers may thus want to send on immediately texts they prepared, or EIS-provided information, to others, without secretarial intervention or an intermediate printout. An extended EIS should provide this convenient, integrated service.

Addresses

One of the most important personal files contains such items as addresses, phone and fax numbers, e-mail addresses, or organisational charts showing employee functions. Managers may want to have immediate access to this kind of information, regardless of time or place, and independent of the services of their secretaries. A more advanced EIS could even provide dialling facilities for telephone, fax, or e-mail, once the address has been retrieved from the files.

Analytical tools

Finally, Executive Information Systems could provide analytical tools to assist more computer-literate and sophisticated managers in more detailed analyses of the information. Managers can select from three different approaches according to the degree to which they work actively with information vis-à-vis computers:

– The *briefing book* approach: managers receive ready-made templates with information, and can navigate from template to template, but without the ability to change information items and information structure as determined in the course of implementation. Managers easily recognise where they are and where they need to go in order to get information within an already familiar structure.

– The *data base* approach: managers are free to navigate in the data base. They can construct their own requests and templates, and form variable relations. At the same time, flexibility can only be achieved through smaller building blocks for the manager, data base entities and records, meaning that access to information is more complex and time consuming.

– The *model-oriented* approach: managers may incorporate data into models, either provided by the EIS or built by the manager according to his or her own plans. This is the approach which the most advanced and computer literate managers may choose in order to make trend extrapolations and simulations, pose what if-questions, and generate effective presentations for meetings and lectures.

Executive systems with these extended services for the manager/user are not just *information* systems. They provide comprehensive computerised support and thus deserve the label *Executive Support System* (Rockart and DeLong 1988).

Executive Information Systems: beyond technology

EIS -- symbolising an information oriented corporate identity

It is often impossible to achieve an exact quantification of the benefits of an EIS. An EIS represents more than quantifiable benefits, it also represents a more conscious and transparent handling of information within each organisation. The main purpose of an EIS is not to provide top-management with an information (and thus power) advantage, but rather to spread information throughout the organisation, to inform others about what the manager deems important. An EIS is designed to let all members of an organisation share the same information important for the organisation. EIS can provide identification with the organisation, *i.e.* organisational consciousness and self-perception. Statistical information such as that concerning students (student numbers, graduates, drop-outs, scores per programme) should be available not only to institutional managers and external statutory bodies, but also to the students at an institution as well.

The "flat" and "loosely coupled" organisational structure of higher education institutions bears the risk of "disorganisation", that those tasks which can only be fulfilled by the institution as a whole are not perceived and handled appropriately. An EIS can provide a shared perception of strengths and weaknesses in the institution as a whole and thus an informational basis for a "corporate identity". In this way, an EIS can be an integral part of a higher education institution's strategic information management.

EIS -- a communication mediator and a communication tool

The "flat" organisation of higher education institutions implies that decisions are made only to a limited extent at its "top". They are made in a "network of decision centres" rather than in a "pyramid structure". "Shared information" provided by an EIS is not only a means of enhancing corporate identity, but is necessary to provide all "centres" of decision-making with the same information base (an "organisational memory") in order to guarantee that coherent decisions are made throughout the institution. An EIS can thus be regarded as a communication base for decision-making in higher education institutions.

Decision-making processes are communication processes. This applies more to "flat" organisations, such as higher education, than to any other organisation. One might therefore conclude that in order to support decision-making in higher education, an EIS should even become a communication tool, rather than just enhancing communication by providing "organisational memory." As mentioned earlier, modern EIS tools can indeed incorporate communication facilitators (see Rockart and DeLong, 1988).

EIS in higher education and the need for co-ordination

"Flat" organisations are far more complex than hierarchical organisations. The higher an organisation's complexity, the greater co-ordination efforts are necessary. In the context of providing higher education institutions with more institutional autonomy, it is often said that central higher education management (chief executive role) should be strengthened, in order to reduce complexity. In industry, where the tendency is towards "flatter" organisational structures, EIS is seen as reducing complexity without giving up the goal of more "loosely coupled" organisational subunits, and thus "flatter" organisations. The existence of information and communication systems alone cannot reduce complexity, and nor can they change organisational structures, but they may assist in coping with the amount of co-ordination needed in such organisations. Through information and communication technology, "we can afford more co-ordination for the same...cost" (Scott Morton, 1991).

How to start with an EIS

The "business problem"

The initial push toward an EIS often begins with a so-called "business problem", perhaps a "unique" problem, which one has not yet seen as such. National discussion might focus on "drop-out rates", and institutional management realises that it knows next to nothing about its own drop-out rates; or budget cuts are expected in the course of budget negotiations with the ministry, and institutional management feels it does not have enough information about its cost structures and performances; or enrolment is falling more at the home institution than the national average, and no information is available about specific reasons.

The business problem may also be a recurring one, such as negotiations to attract a new chairholder to the university. Institutional managers involved in these negotiations should have information about available resources, resources allocated to similar chairs within the institution or at other institutions, and the cost of resources. The push toward an EIS is based on information deficiencies felt by managers, rather than staff member perceptions. Only those staff members who "suffer" from their manager's information exigency will seek gains in efficiency for the collection, transfer, and presentation of information for managerial purposes.

Cost-benefit analysis

Managers should not ask subordinates to start an EIS project with a cost-benefit analysis. If there are sufficient arguments in favour of an EIS, and if managers are convinced of gains with an EIS, a cost benefit analysis cannot reveal anything new. It is more important to undertake a thorough analysis of information processing and communication processes linked to managerial processes in a broader sense. This includes:

- reporting and accountability purposes;
- marketing and public relation purposes; and
- problem identification and problem solving purposes.

It is important to detect where redundancy, multiple data entry, and multiple presentation efforts exist, and where these processes can be made more efficient by combining efforts. The real cost savings of an EIS do not emerge in improved computer user-interface for the manager, a better and faster on-screen presentation of information, but rather in the costs of collecting, transferring, and preparing information for presentation.

The human factor and EIS

The most important prerequisite for an EIS is to find a "sponsor" or "champion", whether a president, vice-president, secretary general, or dean. The sponsor or champion is a potential user of the system. While this person does not need to be a direct end-user, he or she should at least become an intermediate end-user. A champion is the one whose perception of critical success factors is to be implemented in the system. In many cases, a secretary general will be the champion of an EIS. He or she represents the continuous element in higher education management and is responsible for the data already kept in administrative files.

There may be some reluctance on the side of staff members or other institutional managers who do not play the EIS champion role. Those whose task thus far consisted in providing managers with information might fear they will become superfluous, and managers and members of institutional subunits might fear that their realm will become too transparent. An EIS project must begin by convincing everyone within the institution that EIS is not a top-management endeavour, but will serve the whole institution in its efforts to remain competitive and survive.

The software available under the name *Executive Information System* is simply a tool to build the customised EIS of each institution. A lot of analysis and implementation work remains to be done after the first decision to purchase has been made. This service can be bought from external service providers or commissioned to internal personnel. An advantage of having internal project members is that staff members will need to be available for future EIS maintenance.

An EIS does not replace the "information service" personnel. Indeed, to a large extent, an EIS should be fed "automatically" from various internal and external sources. Not only will this "automation" need to be monitored by staff members, domains of EIS information supply will also necessarily change from time to time. New "business problems" cause new information requirements to be incorporated permanently into the system. Finally, as mentioned earlier, an EIS in higher education institutions should be regarded and implemented both as a tool for individual managers as well as an organisational "infrastructure", which itself needs a personnel infrastructure to maintain this EIS "information network" of shared information access and communication facilitators.

Finally, some individual top-manager users may choose to stick to the role of an intermediate end-user only, which should be respected. A secretary or personal assistant knowledgeable about the EIS would then be necessary.

Think big -- start small

Only a short period of time should elapse between the initial EIS idea to the champion's first hands-on experiences. Visions for an EIS might be ambitious, including output and performance-oriented management indicators, external information, and text retrieval and images. It is however important to realise that "cheap" information may be made available very quickly (*e.g.* data from administrative computing systems), and that there is expensive information which is to be "bought" externally or to be generated through surveys.

An EIS should begin with internal information available quickly and at reasonable costs. Many information items are already processed within the institution for public relations and reporting issues. These items, together with data from the administrative computing systems, are the initial information item candidates for an EIS. The EIS should moreover start with those management indicators that were identified in the context of the "business problem". The EIS should not stop with this rather modest and pragmatic initial approach, but move on in the direction of "visions".

The EIS technique

For those managers who decide to become "direct end-users," it is a "must" that the EIS is a PC front-end. In this case, the EIS should be implemented under a graphical user-interface (MS-Windows for MS-DOS, MAC-user interface or Presentation Manager for PS/2 computers). The manager should have a PC on his/her desk in the office, as well as be able to transport the EIS and have it at home. This means that the EIS should also be implemented on a notebook computer to provide users with the same user-interface as in the office environment. The EIS should be filled continuously with actual data. The actual data should be downloaded in short cycles, especially from internal administrative computing files. The manager should also be able to plug the notebook into network services in order to download new information via telephone connection. This is also necessary for linking to e-mail communication channels from wherever the manager and notebook may be.

Conclusions

The *Executive Information System* is the front-end of computerised information services for institutional managers. It supports the systematic use and processing of information in the course of managerial processes, but it also provides managers with access to more informal information and communication channels within and outside the institution, where electronic media are increasingly used.

In higher education, even more than in industry, an EIS does not mean only information supply for individual managers, but rather represents "shared information" for decision-making, here generally made in a decentralised network-like organisational structure. It is therefore important to implement an EIS as a front-end of an informational infrastructure in higher education institutions.

An EIS needs a "champion", both within managerial ranks and within supporting staff. The EIS should begin with internal information available electronically due to information processing in progress. An initial

REFERENCES

Boone, M.E. (1991), *Leadership and the Computer*, Rocklin, CA.

Bud, J. (1991), *Executive Information Systems Management Handbook,* Manchester.

Bullen, C.V. and Rockart, J. F. (1986), "A primer on critical success factors", in Rockart, J. F. and Bullen, C.V. (eds.), *The Rise of Managerial Computing*, Homewood, IL, pp. 383-423.

Burkan, W.C. (1991), *Executive Information Systems -- From Proposal Through Implementation*, New York.

Frackmann, E. (1990), "The revival of management information systems in industry", in *Zeitschrift für Planung*, No. 4, pp. 283-301.

Keen, P.G.W. and Scott Morton, M. (1978), *Decision Support Systems: An Organizational Perspective*, Reading, MA.

Mintzberg, H. (1973), *The Nature of Managerial Work*, Englewood Cliffs, NJ.

Paller, A. and Laska, R. (1990), *The EIS Book: Information Systems for Top Managers,* Homewood, IL.

Rockart, J.F. and DeLong, D.W. (1988), *Executive Support Systems: The Emergence of Top Management Computer Use*, Homewood, IL.

Rockart, J.F. and Flannery, L.S. (1983), "The management of end-user computing: a research perspective", CISR WP, No. 100, Cambridge, MA.

Rockart, J.F. and Treacy, M.E. (1980), "Executive information support systems", CISR WP No. 5, Cambridge, MA.

Scott Morton, M. (1991), *The Corporation of the 1990s: Information Technology and Organizational Transformation*, New York/Oxford.

Thierauf, R.J. (1991), *Executive Information Systems: A Guide for Senior Management and MIS Professionals*, New York.

Figure 5.1. **The context of managerial information in higher education**

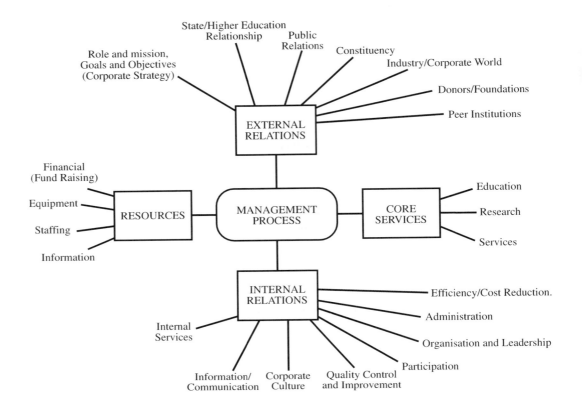

Figure 5.2. **Information categories**

INPUT	PROCESS	OUTPUT

INFORMATION CATEGORIES

Output
Graduates
Employability of Graduates
Quality of Graduates
Salary of Graduates
Prices, Awards, Invitations, Publications
Citations concerning Research
Per Review Results
Research and Services Income
Image

Process
Student/Staff Ratio
Teaching Workload
Duration of Studies
Attrition/Retention/Completion Rates
Ongoing Research Projects
Cost Structures

Internal Environment
Organisational Structure
Internal Service Relations
Organisational Health
Previous Decisions

External Environment
Information on Peer Institutions
Government Decisions, Rules, Regulations, Laws
Information on Donors/Foundations/Other Funding Sources
Data related to Higher Education
Economic Data
Demographic Data
Behaviour and Motivation of Constituents

Input
Financial, Budget Data
Staff
Students, Enrolment
Equipment
Space available and utilised

Chapter 6

THE CHANGING ROLE OF INSTITUTIONAL COMPUTING CENTRES

by

Edgar Frackmann

Introduction

It is appropriate to begin with a brief view of more or less recent developments of computing centres in the corporate world. With computing facilities experiencing a downward drift in prices, and with an increasing need for computing power in whatever corner of the respective business organisation, the concentration of facilities into one computing centre has dissolved. Computing "centres" flourished like mushrooms throughout the company. In this process, computing power not only came closer to users and respective user departments, but the overall company-wide responsibility for an IT policy disappeared as well.

Recently, an opposite trend seems to be arising. A range of reports in journals and newspapers, as well as scientific research, discuss a consolidation of computing centres, *i.e.* dispersed computing centres are being locally concentrated with regard to the number of computers and personnel. Sometimes the consolidation is only a first step to "outsource" the computing facilities and their management. At the same time, responsibility for information resources policy is becoming re-integrated and moving upwards in company decision-making hierarchies.

The following main reasons are given to justify re-centralisation measures:

– increasing costs of decentralised (and duplicated) expertise (human resources) that is needed to operate and maintain the computing facilities;

– the opportunity to limit the number of software licences, due to both a reduction of licences and a joint purchasing power in meeting the software suppliers;

– the decrease of transmission cost and remote access to data, which makes it increasingly irrelevant where data are stored and maintained; and

– finally, the increasing role of the information and communication technology infrastructure, *i.e.* the information resources infrastructure works for the competitiveness of the organisations. In this context, the need to provide standards and rules while investing in and applying technology increases.

It would be an over-simplification to regard these re-centralisation processes as just a wave, where decentralisation is followed by a phase of centralisation, which might again be followed by another decentralisation phase. What appears as re-centralisation turns out to combine the advantages of decentralisation with the pay-offs of centralisation in terms of both costs and service orientation. Access to computing resources and data remains as close to the customer as has been achieved in the decentralisation phase. Decentralised departments retain their decision-making authority on the extent to which they use the services of central-service providers (profit centres, outsourcers, or other central in-house units). At the same time, certain computing and human resources (specialised experts), as well as the responsibility for the IT infrastructure, are highly centralised in these organisation models.

In terms of higher education, these developments in the corporate world demonstrate that there are three main criteria which should guide the organisational models for the institutional computing centres in higher education:

- the cost of services related to information and communication technology according to the different organisation models of the service provision;

- the quality of services; and

- the infrastructural and strategic character of the respective IT components.

Guided by these criteria, the following sections will deal with the functions of a more or less central organisational unit in higher education focusing on IT, structural models for the fulfilment of these functions and resourcing models, and finally, management problems related to these functions. This paper is meant as a management briefing more for the general management of higher education institutions than for IT management. The latter might not find any new information in this paper, because it is an attempt to reflect on the very process and problems with which they are often confronted. This paper is based on discussions from an OECD/IMHE workshop of experts. All participants (except for the author of this paper) are upper-level managers of institutional computing centres (or whatever these organisational units are called today).

The functions of the "new computing centres"

As the name "Computing Centre" indicates, these organisational units, within higher education institutions, used to be responsible for the operation of the institution's central computing facilities -- previously the main computing facilities available to the various departments and members who needed computing power. But more and more often decentralised organisational units, like departments, institutes, chairs, laboratories, library, and administration, purchased, operated and maintained their computing facilities themselves. They thus increasingly asked, why they need a computing *centre* at all. Behind general doubts about central units, of course, is the idea that whatever resources (budgets, personnel) are located centrally, they could be deployed to the decentralised user units. Costs of services and facilities, aside from the service quality, might indeed be better, the closer service providers are to users, the more users may have their fingers on the service provision. Or to put it another way, users will accept whatever level of service, the more they feel that they are being served by their own service providers.

To pose this radical question means starting from scratch in terms of functions of a central unit and its responsibilities. The questions to be raised are twofold:

– Are there any IT *facilities* which, for the sake of cost reduction or because of their centrality to institutional strategy or infrastructural character, should rather be subsumed under central responsibility and centrally-maintained operation?

– Are there any *services* which, for the sake of cost reduction and level of service quality, should be given into the hands of a central organisational unit instead of leaving it with the users themselves?

Facilities

Campus network

Infrastructure is always a third choice. But, networks are the computers of the future. The campus network is the necessary infrastructure for all those who are dependent on such network services, as communication, file transfer, remote access to specialised computing facilities. Not only the network itself, but also value-adding services, come under the responsibility of the institutional computing centre. If there is a facility which needs centralised responsibility and operation, a corporate plan, co-ordination or agreements on standards, then it is the campus network with its gateways and servers to the external world (like domain name server *e.g.*). The campus network thus comes quite naturally under the responsibility of a computing *centre* of a higher education institution. It would be far too expensive for each organisational subunit of an institution to be provided with its own access to national and international research networks.

Peak capacities

Investment in IT might follow two different policies: 1) investment according to needed capacities of the respective computing facility and computing power, or 2) investment for provision of certain computing facilities. The latter investment policy, which reflects the most decentralised decision-making on IT investment, might lead to overhead capacity, wherever certain computing facilities are thought to be needed. In order to reduce overall investment in IT, the computing centre could take on the role of providing peak capacity. This might apply to central multi-user computers, servers, workstations, student-focused PC or workstation pools, or specialised facilities like high resolution colour printers.

Latest technology

The danger clearly exists that a single decentralised unit will not fully utilise the latest technology. Computing centres might take on an innovative function to promote the latest technology for public use within the institution, and finally to prepare its own staff to meet future requirements. While it might be too expensive to adjust all PC or workstation pools continuously to the latest technology, the computing centre could have the task of keeping pace with technological development for one central computer pool. Computer centres should exercise some caution about what is only visible in the dawn of technological invention, but ensure not to be too late in promoting those technologies and results of international standardisation efforts. Today, for example this applies to multi-media mail, X-500 directories and CD-ROM technology accessing multi-media information.

High performance computing

It is perhaps dangerous to see responsibility for high performance computing facilities as the main justification for an institutional computing centre. High performance computing is not general purpose computing; that is, only a limited number of specialist users need high performance computing facilities. These computing facilities may easily absorb 30 per cent and more of investment budgets and personnel resources of a computing centre, without serving a similar proportion of overall users. The significant issue is whether high performance computing should be part of the computer centre budget, or whether it should instead be part of the big science budgets. The operation of high performance computers may well come under the responsibility of the computer centre, but it should be made clear that this does not represent the core function of the "new computing centre".

Services

This is the most striking new role of the new computing centre. From its former responsibility of running centrally-available hardware, it shifted to a *service centre* for hardware and software, irrespective of its location within the institution. Clearly, the computer centre staff has to learn that there are IT experts everywhere in the institution. Compared to some 15 years ago, every IT user is to a certain extent an expert. Within the university there are places where people know the IT job, especially its innovative function, better than those in the computer centre. But an increasing number of users do not want to go into details with IT; they want to call on experts when the technology does not seem user-friendly. Another species of organisational subunits within the institutions do afford an excessive amount of routine or exception-oriented administration with regard to IT. Their time and efforts could better be assigned to their primary task of teaching and research of each unit.

The new computing centre should provide or handle access to experts outside the institution for whatever situation might arise. The computing centre should be assigned the routine administration of the decentralised computing facilities wherever this helps reduce the overall personnel capacity devoted to these tasks in a higher education institution. This concentration of knowledge, capacities, and contact points to external partners may reduce both internal personnel costs and the cost of external services and products to be purchased outside the institution.

General user support -- the Help Desk

The Help-Desk is the general entry point for an institution's IT users for problems of all sorts. The help-desk staff possesses a broad knowledge, especially in those technologies most used within the institution. But the help-desk people cannot know everything. They have to know where to get an answer for the user, and they have to make sure that the answer is found for the user, whether they transfer the solution to the user or the user to the expert. The success of a computer centre's help-desk determines its service orientation, and will contribute significantly to the acceptance of such a central organisational unit. In some cases, it might be necessary that the help-desk staff not only inform the user what to do to solve the problem but to support the user throughout the problem solving process. This certainly applies to the computer facilities directly within the computer centre's realm of responsibility. Whether it also applies to user-owned computer facilities depends on the extent to which the computing centre is able to provide users with additional services, far beyond consulting and toward total services.

Services for the user facilities

In this new environment of decentralised computing, users have their own computer facilities which, at first glance, have nothing to do with equipment in other parts of the institution. Users or user departments may purchase equipment out of their own budgets, based on their own expertise, install the hardware and software themselves and even plug it into a campus network. Users may have their own maintenance contracts with suppliers or do the maintenance themselves, and they may have their own troubleshooting and consulting people and mechanisms, including manuals and documentation.

For the sake of reducing personnel cost, or to lower prices for hardware and software and external services, all these services may be concentrated in the hands and responsibility of a computing centre.

Purchasing

The computer centre may have the task of maintaining vendor relations, including market and product analyses and comparisons. Recommendations for users may be derived from this market scanning and testing of hardware and software, as well as contracts with vendors in order to get better prices for institutional members and sub-organisations. Under the general heading of purchasing, the computer centre could also operate a micro-computer shop with not only PCs and workstations, but also software, periphery, and all accessories needed to run a computer and networks. The computer shop deserves significant attention, especially if there is a student- owned computing policy of the institution. In this context, it becomes evident that the institution's users are not only such sub-organisations, as departments, institutes, chairs and laboratories, but also individual users who purchase their equipment out of their individual pockets. Especially in educational institutions, and to the same extent for teachers/researchers and students, the distinction between work and leisure, home and office, is blurring, and this must be reflected in central services provision as well.

The purchasing job of a computer centre may also include the negotiation of software licences (bulk and site licences). There is no doubt that this task includes standardisation decisions (to be dealt with later in this chapter).

Installation

Installation, including plugging equipment into the campus network in order to benefit from network services, may be a routine job. For users, however, who do not always handle the installation of their computers, this can be time-consuming and even a waste of time, considering their primary task in teaching and research. There are many users in an institution who are not willing to plunge deeply into the computer configuration. They want to have access to their local applications, to network services, and remote information and applications. They want to be *users*. For a growing number of institutional members, the computer centre can provide a highly valuable service in the installation, configuration and consulting services connected to PCs, workstations and sub-networks, including the connection to the campus network and its services.

Maintenance

The central maintenance service of the computing centre can provide both its own personnel, with special expertise in maintenance areas, such as repair and provision of intermediate replacements, and institution-wide maintenance contracts for certain widely-used hardware and software components.

Competency centre and information exchange

For all kinds of generally and widely- used hardware and software, the computing centre may be the competence centre and organise the exchange of information. Computing centre staffs should be informed about such areas as new versions and releases of software, software bugs, common interfaces between software products, product lines of hardware vendors, and about internal or external information files and services available via the campus network. This specialised knowledge might reach into the domain of applications, especially those applications widely used on campus, like office automation, communication and other standard software. Information exchange and transfer might be organised through consulting and troubleshooting services (help desk), centrally-provided training courses, through printed or electronically-delivered documentation, and public announcements.

Total services

The campus network can be used to provide for users upon request, with a total services package for their computing facility connected to the network. The user may embed his or her machine into a remote control, remote maintenance, remote booting and a remote back-up service, a service package provided by the computer centre. This service might include providing the user with centrally-purchased software to be downloaded to his or her computer only for the period of applying the software. Apart from its service perspective , this feature, of course, limits the number of needed licences on campus and reduces the overall software cost. This measure, however, clearly needs central co-ordination through the campus software policy.

Organisational memory

Organisational memory consists of both recent and past relevant information. Past information is usually represented by an institution's archives, preserving all kinds of important incoming and outgoing mail, as well as important documents like Senate or committee decisions. Increasingly, this past information will be kept in electronic form, and computing centres could become responsible for maintaining electronic archives. Another part of the organisational memory consists in holding information for immediate access, such as that relevant to students and courses, committees, press releases for an internal audience, and address files. Again, this information will be made accessible on-line from each of the front-ends in the campus network. The question is whether the computer centre should be responsible for the electronic provision of this information, thus providing another value-added service on the campus network.

Relationships

Another issue is whether the new computing centre is still concerned with information and communication *technology,* or whether *information resources* equally fall within its responsibilities. One might distinguish three layers in dealing with information resources in the institutional context:

- use of information;
- information systems (applications); and
- IT infrastructure.

The use of information in higher education has two dimensions: 1) handling information in the context of primary processes (*i.e.* teaching, learning, and research), and 2) supporting processes such as the library, management and administration. Information systems are the applications to support users in handling the information, like administrative computing systems, information retrieval systems, CAI/CAL to support the teaching and learning process, communication software like e-mail, and software used to support research. Finally, the IT infrastructure consists of computers, servers, and networks.

The question is whether the new computing centre's tasks should and could be restricted to maintaining the IT infrastructure. As mentioned earlier, the computing centre could be made responsible for maintaining the organisational memory, it also could be made responsible to purchase standard software. One of the value-added services of the campus network is to provide access to internal and external information. Finally, it should be an urgent task of the computer centre to provide a common user interface for all these services, and thus to provide a generic application. With the shift from a computing centre to a service provider, it is apparent that the boundaries between the three layers are becoming blurred, and the user interface example makes it clear that the distinction between infrastructure and application is no longer decisive. In light of this development, it is necessary to recognise that the new computing centre is entering the realm of other service units within the higher education institution, at the same time when other organisational units might be seeking a field of service offerings where the computer centre might presumably take on an active role.

Institutional information resources policy and organisation need to address how to solve this problem, how to organise co-operation and co-ordination, as well as how to avoid duplication and costly overlapping. There are a number of organisational units, service centres, or information resources to be regarded in this context:

Library

The library, of course, is one of the most important co-ordinators for information resources in the teaching and research environment of higher education. For the present purpose, the library means both the central institutional library and decentralised libraries, as well as access to regional and national libraries. Due to the campus network and regional and national research networks, a virtual library is emerging for students and researchers. The OPAC (On-line Public Access Catalogue) clearly is a value-added service on the campus network. Librarians also might feel responsible for providing institution members with access to national and international data bases, both on-line and CD-ROM based. They also feel that it is necessary to organise an electronic document delivery system via the campus network, to add software to the information resources, stored and delivered by the library, such as software for text analysis. Organisational memory and campus-wide information systems might also come under the responsibility of an institutional library. The library is changing from guarding books on shelves to an information services provider. There is, at least, necessarily a close co-operation between the library and the new computing centre in order to achieve synergy of institutional resources co-ordination rather then duplication and costly animosity.

Administrative computing

Central institutional administrations and management were "emancipated" from institutional computing centres some 15 or 20 years ago, with the installation of their own mainframes for administrative computing systems and management information systems. In a sense, this is to be seen in the context of the decentralisation process of computing in higher education institutions, in terms of departments, institutes, chairs, laboratories, and finally, the library, each with its own computing facilities. Administrative computing itself experienced a decentralisation process when central administration mainframes were displaced by computers dedicated to such different administrative domains, such as accounting, student ad ministration, personnel, and physical plant, each with its own computers. In addition, various areas of the decentralised administration, including the departments, institutes, research projects, were installing hardware and software in order to support and automate their own administrative processes. In order to develop and use the full potential of computerisation for institutional administration and management, all these computer islands have to be linked through the campus network, or a separate administrative network with well-defined and protected gateways to the campus network and its services (including communication servers for the external world).

Public access to administrative data and information (be it entry or retrieval) will emerge as one of the most important issues to be tackled in the future of administrative computing and related network issues. The central administration, as well as decentralised administrative units, should not boost their staff-numbers in order for each of them to have their own network specialist group. After two decades of separation, both the new computing centre and the administrative computing groups will have to find new modes of co-operation.

Audio-visual services and computer-aided learning and teaching units

In many institutions, there are no central supporting units for audio-visual teaching and learning systems or for CAI/CAL. Audio-visual services may well be organised very decentrally (*e.g.* on an institute or chair basis with one person responsible for only the user time- table of the equipment). CAI/CAL might also be dealt with in a research context rather than by a centrally responsible service unit within a higher education institution. One can however, identify a need for a central service in order to exploit fully the benefits of new computerised facilities for the teaching and learning processes. Again, it is a question of concentrating resources and efforts so that at least a close co-operation between educational support units and the new computing centre be organised.

Telephone

The tendency towards only one network to serve the transmission of data, voice images, and video will also lead to the organisation of joint responsibility for this network. Today the maintenance of the campus network and telephone systems is often found in different service units of the higher education institution.

IT policy -- information resources policy

Information resources -- the computer-supported use, handling, and transmission of information -- have become vital to the success of higher education institutions, and consumes a large amount of financial and personal resources. Institutions need an information resources policy and management. IT infrastructure and information systems, investments, operation, and maintenance must be planned, co-ordinated, monitored, and continuously adjusted. Decisions have to be made which deal with the whole of the institution rather than with only separate parts.

The computing centre or its chief manager might not be the organisational unit or individual to make these decisions; rather, committees, the senate, or top institutional management teams will take on this responsibility. These decision-making bodies need the expertise of the computing centre and its staff. The computing centre staff has the task to prepare the decisions of these committees and decision-making bodies, to draft institutional IT plans, investment policies, and information services policies. There are several issues where the information resources policy support of the new computing centre is needed:

IT infrastructure

Above all else, the campus network requires continuous planning and decision-making with regard to such areas as investment, standards, and funding. Moreover, how to time the promotion and implementation of new technology on a centralised basis is a decision for the new computing centre with its expertise and judgement about technological developments.

Organisation

The organisation of information resources, *i.e.* whether services are centralised or decentralised, whether bought or self-made are issues for institutional decision-making bodies. The new computing centre could weigh the pros and cons of different options.

Standardisation

Standards can save money and personnel resources, facilitate the use of IT, and enable users to benefit from the computing centre's services and the value-added services on the campus network. Standards provide the links among users. Standards also provide the institutions' access to national and international information sources. One of the tasks of the new computing centre is to promote and prepare decisions about IT standards and to develop such institution-specific standards as common user interfaces for all services available through the campus network. At the same time, however, the computing centre has to cope with the tension between the stability, continuity, and security seemingly guaranteed by standards, on the one hand, and the need for innovation with its attendant risks and moments of deviation and non-conformity on the other.

Controlling

In spite of falling prices for IT components, an increasing proportion of institutional budgets seem to be committed to information resources. This may reflect not only the importance of IT for the institutional role and mission, but also requires increasing scrutiny of cost structure and proportions. Decisions about organisational alternatives have to be based on sound analysis, and users must be convinced that the most efficient solutions also provide for the best service level and quality. Users should not take IT-related services for granted, but be aware of the costs incurred by information and communication technology. It may be the continuous task of the computing centre to generate this information and make it available to a wider audience, including decision-makers.

A new name for the new computing centre

Based on the previous description, it is clear that the functions of institutional computing centres have changed significantly, from focusing on hardware to an increasing emphasis on service. Knowledge, expertise, and human capital are more important for the computing centre than the computing facilities for which it is responsible. Only part of the total institutional computing facilities belong to the computing centre, but the computing centre needs to possess expert knowledge of almost all components of the institutional IT infrastructure. From its main concern with the stability, security, and continuity of IT infrastructure, the computing centre took on another commitment to innovation and dynamism, and a shift towards service including an openness to technological development.

The *Computing Centre* is no longer the right name for the organisational unit under discussion. Not the computing task, but *services* determine the character of this central unit. Thus, a better name would be *Information resources service centre* or the like.

The computer-related tasks of the new computing centre, or the information resources service centre, are far more complex than those of the previous single-unit-multi- purpose mainframe era. Today, it has to cope with a heterogeneous computer and network environment with facilities spread across campuses. This represents less a physical computing centre than a logical, virtual computing centre. As the main resources of the new computing centre are less hardware and more human resources, due to its service character, the main parameters of success and performance are not hardware and software investment, but organisation and investment in knowledge and expertise.

There are many who advocate a return of the new computing centres to the laboratory type organisation (institute for applied computer science), *i.e.* their origin and role before they became computing centres. One should take into account, however, that these central units owe their existence to their role as service centres where the skills, knowledge and expertise should be directed mainly to provide different IT users of the institution with viable and reliable IT-related services according to their different needs. Once endowed, however, with this high level of knowledge and expertise, the new computing centre clearly has the task to prepare the paths, strategies, and policies for the implementation and use of new technologies within the institutional framework, *e.g.* while conducting and promoting exploratory research.

If not hardware, but organisation and human resources are the main determinants of a successful and valuable computing centre, then these issues equally need examination. The following sections of this paper are devoted first to structure and issues of resourcing, and second to the management and staffing issues of the new computing centres.

Structure and resourcing

While dealing with the new computing centres -- the information resources service centres -- that rely more on their human capital than on technology, structure and organisation are more important issues than technology. There is of course no one single structure and resourcing model for information resources services. It might however be useful that an organisation, such as the university, is ready and willing to re-organise from time to time, not only to cope with routine-related inertia, and the emergence of costly niches (if an organisation is not continuously scrutinised), but also with rapid developments in the field of information and communication technology, which itself might have ramifications for the organisational structure and resourcing models.

Organisational alternatives

Since no single ideal organisational structure for information resources services exists, it is interesting to follow the "history" of emerging organisation models and to try to identify their underlying criteria and rational.

Structure according to technical tasks

In the period when the computing centre (its services and self-perception) was mainly influenced by the central computing facilities it provided for an entire institution, technical criteria and technology-related tasks had more of an influence on the shape of its organisation. A typical organisational structure often made distinctions among the following departments, groups, or division of responsibilities:

- *Systems:* Responsibility for the different operation systems, like the mainframe operating system, mini-computer operating systems, and finally Unix.

- *Applications:* This group would take care of applications operated and manifested by the computing centre such as programming languages, standard software packages and graphical software. It could also be made responsible for the software of adjacent services, such as library and administrative computing software.

- *Networking:* Installing, supporting, and maintaining the campus network or local networks as required by users is the task of another group of the institutional computing centre.

- *Maintenance:* Another group could itself be in charge of maintenance or could organise maintenance in contracts with hardware and software suppliers.

- *Operations:* This group could consist of the centrally-installed equipment operators, whether the mainframe, workstations, PCs, or network servers.

– *User Services:* Apart from technical tasks, the user comes into view. A special organisational subunit is the contact point for users, whether mainframe, network, workstation, or PC users, those who use the computing centre facilities, as well as those who have their own equipment.

Structure according to facilities

Users work with different facilities. While some are central (*i.e.* belong to the computing centre), others are departmental or even personal (PCs and workstations). An organisational structure oriented more toward user facilities, and which appreciates the decentralisation of computing facilities, can be structured to distinguish among the following responsibilities of different groups or departments:

– networking;
– mainframe computer;
– distributed systems; and
– personal systems.

User services structure

Finally, a third organisational structure would most obviously reflect the development of the central computing centre towards a central service unit. This organisation is characterised by only a few operating groups, one responsible for the campus network and another for centrally or de-localised servers or pools belonging the computing centre.

Another group within this organisation brings together specialists with different fields and areas of expertise, such as Unix specialists, local area network specialists, and PC or MAC specialists. There are not only technology specialists, but also those experts in purchasing support, maintenance organisation and support, and information services access support.

The third building block of this services-oriented organisation structure reflects the user groups formed by the organisational substructure of the institution itself (faculties, schools, and departments). There may be different supporting units for the arts and humanities, economies and social sciences, natural sciences, and engineering. This third component of the services oriented organisation structure might best consider the implications of decentralised computer facilities, and, to a certain extent, the decentralisation of knowledgeability about IT.

The question is if and to what extent this third organisational building block should be part of the computing centre at all, or rather part of the user organisation -- the respective department, school, institute, or laboratory. There are many reasons which favour a certain autonomy from, or a looser-coupling, with the computing centre.

One reason for this partition of user services, and the partially decentralised responsibility for IT users, is found in the fact that many user organisations, such as departments, have developed their own IT specialists who already play a certain role in user services in their respective units. The computing centre cannot survive by doing something that everyone else in the institution can do alone. However, the computing centre could rely on the personnel and competence structures, and provide for liaison units within the computing centre of the decentralised IT areas. A hidden agenda would be to join the central staff with IT experts located in the departments, in order to achieve a good balance between keeping things together and sufficient fragmentation. A user service, which the user may identify as one's own service, is a guarantee that the institutional information resources policies will be implemented throughout the institution. It is thus a loose but co-ordinated structure, a co-ordinated decentralisation of IT support. The tasks of managing the institutional IT services thus come to resemble conducting an orchestra rather than hierarchical command and execution.

One should keep in mind that while promoting such a network-like organisation structure as in information resources *services*, the overall institutional *information resources policy* -- the institutional information management -- may not be decentralised.

Decision-making

Each institution might have a decision-making body, such as an information management board, consisting of the rector, the computing centre director, or the CIO (chief information resources officer), the user representatives, and other information-related service units, such as the library, administration, and educational service units.

It might be worthwhile to mention that this decision-making body deals not only with the investments and task organisation of the computing centre, but also with the whole institutional information management, including standards, licensing policy, information resources architecture, and common user interfaces. They decide on an institution-wide strategy plan for information resources, perhaps based on the expertise of the new computing centre.

What is also important is that the decisions have a two-fold focus: first, that the institutional information resources policy and strategy guarantee that the institution keep pace with technological developments; second, that IT users are best served in their daily demands on their own and central computing facilities. It might be advantageous to have users represented in the central decision-making bodies, and that they have their own user committees to make sure that IT users are served according to the proportion of budget devoted to IT.

The CIO role

Whether a higher education institution should have a CIO, a chief information resources officer, is often linked to the question whether all information resources- related organisation units within the institution should report to one chief administrator. This would mean that units like the computing centre, library, administrative computing group, and IT-related education service units, would be put under one umbrella, an information resources centre directed by the CIO.

Here, it is appropriate recall the image of the orchestra. Co-ordination can exist without a traditional hierarchical command and reporting structure. What seems to be important is that co-ordination takes place, not that there is a unified organisation. This "orchestra" can be expanded (where central and decentralised experts play together in order to serve IT users) to include the library, administrative computing, and CAI/CAL experts.

Apart from expert players, we need a "conductor". There are strong arguments that a CIO role is necessary in higher education institutions because the co-ordination and concentration of IT-related efforts is vital. Decisions concerning the institutional information resources strategy are already made by committees or the information resources board. But, these decisions have to be prepared. Someone needs to be the guardian of technological promotion and innovation, especially with regard to the institutional IT infrastructure, someone to guide decisions as to when and how to enter new technologies, someone to organise IT-related services for the whole organisation.

The CIO could be a vice-rector or vice-president, responsible for the information resources infrastructure of the institution, or the computing centre director, who is made a member of the institution's chief management team.

Co-ordination mechanisms and resourcing

Users need to rely on the information resources-related services for their primary tasks. The question is to be raised as to how the co-ordination between service provision and service consumption should be organised. Co-ordination mechanisms have something to do with the question of who should pay for what. One might differentiate four alternative models with regard to co-ordination and resourcing mechanisms for IT-related user services:

Central provision of services

In this model, users are not asked whether or not they need services. Services are available and are not to be paid for by the users, but are budgeted centrally (top-sliced). One might call this co-ordination and resourcing model the infrastructural approach. It was formerly the usual model for the mainframe era of institutional computing centres, and it continues to be applied to the basic network infrastructure. This model provides equitable access to the respective facilities, and it is a co-ordination and resourcing model for promoting information and communication technology use within the institution.

This model has, however, one major disadvantage. There is a danger that users and service providers become increasingly alienated from each other. Because service providers have secure funding, they may devote their efforts to technology rather than to users, who sense that the service organisation is not *their* service unit. The users would often prefer to use this centrally-allocated money at their own decentralised discretion. Indeed, the popularity of this model is waning, and is being replaced by what might be called:

Do-it-yourself

Users often react to these deficiencies with the conviction that they are best served if services are provided out of their own resources, meaning not only their own budget but their own personnel and facilities as well. Indeed, the closer a service is to the user, the better it may be adjusted and customised to user needs. But, this is also an expensive model, unless it is combined with central backup of expertise and capacities. This model implies that whatever, wherever, and whenever the capacity is needed, it will be provided, and this can as a whole result in a tremendous overhead for the institution. An alternative might be to purchase services only to the extent that they are really needed at a given time. This model has an appropriate name:

Market model

The market model implies that the full amount of services are charged to users. It generally does not make a difference whether services are provided from within the institution or from outside suppliers. A fully-developed market model would however mean that the user chooses between inside and outside suppliers, and that the suppliers are not restricted as to whom they offer services.

It seems quite evident that for the majority of software used in the institution, the market model is the best option. There also exist cases where mainframes, the operation of the institutional network, and high performance facilities are not the task of a central service unit but of an *outside resource* provider (outsourcing) where the outsourcers emerged out of national, regional, or joint institutional computing centres.

In the market model the user may buy the service needed; and the service has to be paid out of the user's budget. Service providers are forced to maintain a high level of service quality in order not to lose their customers and to survive. There is still the danger that if there is no market, there is no service. One remaining model tries to combine the reliability of user services, and close user-proximity with secure access to necessary expertise, availability of peak capacity, and implementation and ad ministration of a joint institutional information resources policy. This model is called:

Network organisation

If an institution does not wish to charge for services and apply a market-like co-ordination and resourcing mechanism, but still aims at a closer relation of demand and resources, it must convince the user to devote a certain amount of resources to IT services. Users have to become involved in *their* services, to devote *their* money to *their* own services, while keeping services well-co-ordinated. They should feel that they have their own service units and control over their funds. This model is best implemented if the user organisation (*i.e.* the department, school, etc.) has its own personnel to support users and as an immediate contact for IT-related problem-solving. There might be one or more persons per department according to the intensity of IT use, or two or more departments might share resources to have one IT expert.

These user-funded support units must, however, have their equivalent in the computing centre, *i.e.* the central service providers. Both work closely together. In this way, one can involve knowledgeable users with the institution's information resources policy and eliminate hostility between users and the computing centre, and provide users with a more comprehensive service than would be the case with totally decentralised services (*i.e.* the "do-it-yourself" model). Users also have to be aware that IT services come at a certain cost. The network model is well suited to promote this awareness. The users themselves decide how many resources to devote to their IT services.

The network organisation model seems very valuable for higher education settings and deserves to be elaborated in more detail for the future of information resources services in higher education.

Co-operation between computing centres

A special issue concerning the organisation of a computing centre is if, and to what extent, it should seek co-operation with other computing centres. In most countries, computing centres have set up something like an association in order to organise the exchange of information and oftentimes lobbying. This may occur on a more or less formal basis, with more or less stable structures, on a permanent or project basis, in order to investigate major challenges to the computing centres. Apart from these more general organisational liaisons, there are many reasons why computing centres should co-operate with each other on an individual basis.

Outsourcing

An institutional computing centre cannot and perhaps should neither provide experts and expertise for everything nor offer everything. It can offer more focused services and a higher service level if it can rely on co-operating computing centres, their services, and specialised resources for other services. In the case of outsourcing, it is of course possible that co-operation turns into competition. Outsourcers have to survive in the market of IT-related services and thus may easily enter competition with institutional computing centres. Competition often, however, contributes to lowering prices of services and augmenting service quality.

Peak capacities

Co-operation among computing centres may also be used to provide the optimal general purpose capacity or specific computing facilities on a mutual basis.

Contingency planning

Due to the network infrastructure, institutional computing facilities and network infrastructure can easily be operated and monitored from a remote place. Thus, computing centres may help each other when unforeseen personnel vacancies and shortages arise.

Evaluation of service quality

Evaluating the service quality of the new computing centres is a very difficult endeavour. It starts by defining more or less measurable quality criteria. One way to evaluate service quality is to form peer auditing groups, members of other computing centres who investigate the services of each different centre in a peer review process. Computing centres thus may help each other to improve their services for the sake of their respective customers.

Management and staffing issues

The manager individual

Managing the new computing centre and its subunits clearly requires technical expertise and a solid knowledge basis. Although it deals with technology, the new computing centre, is a service centre, and managers have to understand the service job and be able to motivate their staff as excellent technologists who have a sense of what service orientation means.

It seems very important that computing centre managers, of whatever management level, have the opportunity to attend management courses focusing on this new service culture. There are examples of managers who try better to understand the users, their customers, by themselves engaging in service, for example, as consultants at the help-desk service for a couple hours a week.

The new computing centre managers have to rely on a hybrid of technical and management expertise, and practical experiences and skills. One model to cope with these requirements is to have two directors of the new computing centre, one focused on technology, the other on administration and business. Still, both have to understand the new job of the computing centre as a service unit.

Organisation and relationships

One task for the new computer centre managers is to promote the organisation of IT- related services, dealt with in the last section. This whole process of organisation is based on the factual decentralisation of equipment, decision-making, and knowledge. The computing centre no longer has a monopoly on computers, power in this field, and IT-related skills and knowledge. Tensions, if not animosity, arise between academics and computer centre professionals. Academics tend to focus only on their own business, to ignore the necessity of corporate plans and institutional allegiance, whereas the computing centre and its managers represent the whole of the institutional information resources policy and strategy.

Computing centre managers have to try to dissolve the borders between researchers and professionals. They cannot dictate standards and measures to serve the efficient provision of IT-related services. They need to encourage and convince, and then finally need to market the services of their centres, perhaps best accomplished by a convincing quality of service.

One way to dissolve the tension, animosity, and misunderstanding is to involve academics in computer centre meetings, working groups, and expert meetings. It seems vital that IT-knowledgeable users in particular are active in policy and operating decisions of the computing centre.

Service orientation

Whether the computing centre services are billed or not, their existence and budget are under permanent review and scrutiny. The users of the former mainframe computing centre developed into customers of a service provider. One of the most important management issues is to assure that computing centre members have the right service orientation, and to provide a visible service culture.

The first issue is that the computer centre should know what services and service standards are required by customers. There are two dimensions to be considered concerning the kind of required services. One can be derived from technological development and the tasks to be fulfilled by higher education institution. The other is influenced by specific users, their behaviour, knowledge, previous standards, institutional traditions, and cultures. Knowledge about what the users need, and getting them involved in the definition and provision of services, are best generated through the network organisation model described above. Managers and members of the new computing centre have to listen to users, and then combine their wishes with what is needed based on institutional strategies and policies.

The second issue is that service levels and standards should be stated publicly. Users should know what they can expect from the new computing centre, and service providers should know to what they are committed. This kind of publicity about computing centre activities might also contribute to a better understanding among institutional members about what the new computing centre means.

The third problem is to turn this kind of service orientation and service culture into an inherent component of each individual job in the new computing centre, and to achieve a service commitment of each individual. This might be one of the most important and difficult jobs for the new computing centre managers, to "cultivate" service orientation.

The fourth issue of service orientation is finally how to assess, or better to measure, the service quality of the computing centre. If service criteria are stated in the form of a checklist, or even in measurable standards, of what was described as a first issue of service orientation, then it should be possible to assess progress toward these goals. Still it remains a very difficult endeavour. At least two kinds of quality assessment are imaginable: the peer review, and customer surveys. One should, however, bear in mind that the best assurance of quality is to prevent quality deficiencies, rather than to detect and remedy deficiencies *ex post*.

Staffing issues

Staff, not technical equipment, is the real source of the new computing centre as a service unit. Management efforts thus have to emphasize staffing and organisational problems. The problem is that a considerable proportion of today's institutional computing centre staff was hired some 20 years ago. The computing centre might also be burdened with some of the most routine (if not boring) jobs left in the IT world. A certain inertia and indolence in organisational niches have also emerged over the years, accompanied by conflicts with challenges to the new computing centre to keep pace with technological developments and service requirements.

The computing centre must have a significant budget for training, continuing education, and sending its staff to conferences, in order to make them write papers and learn communication skills with both customers and colleagues. With a majority of staff hired years ago, it might be useful to hire (perhaps even on a part time basis) some young people and put them into departments where they could "motivate by example".

Computing centre staff should not compete with users and their knowledge. They should concentrate on specific subjects, on what is needed beyond a user's knowledge and skills. Computing centre managers should try to break the "guru culture". Knowledge should no longer be regarded as an ingredient for power, but to be acquired in order to be transferred and used in the context of service provision.

Technical staff of the computing centre should rotate through the help-desk services. Computing centre staff must be brought to the users. This might be organised through rotation, hospitality, or recruitment of computing centre staff from user departments. Central and decentralised IT staff have to be co-ordinated and brought together in the context of the network organisation.

It might be necessary to assure that not all staff members of the computing centre be localised centrally. Equipment belonging to the computing centre can be installed closer to user departments, as well as personnel, in order to take charge of operating and maintaining the respective (decentralised) computing facilities and serving local users.

Conclusions

Many of the issues and problems dealt with here should be solved within computing centres. Customising functions and services, organisation, staffing, and cultivating service orientation, are all part of the task facing the new computing centre managers. General managers of higher education institutions should be familiar with the internal problems of computing centres when deciding if and how the services under review should be provided: centrally, decentrally, outsourced, top-sliced, or charged. They should also identify functional management tasks and challenges, while selecting managers for the new computing centre, if not the CIO.

Chapter 7

IMPLEMENTING AN INFORMATION STRATEGY
The case of the Vienna University of Economics and Business Administration

by

Barbara Sporn and Georg Miksch
Vienna University of Economics and Business Administration, Austria

Strategic information systems planning at *Wirtschaftsuniversität Wien* (WU) is used to solve problems related to mass higher education. The WU is the federal University of Economics and Business Administration located in Vienna, Austria, and represents the largest European university for business studies, enrolling around 20 000 students each year. Given the mission of WU to become the leading business school in Europe, this goal can only be reached by drastically reducing the administrative work load of all university members.

University-wide software as well as hardware standards, enormous investments in modem technology as well as end-user focused marketing and training represent the milestones of WU's information strategy. Innovative projects for implementing this strategy at WU are often sponsored by the computer industry. A new label called *Power* was created to enhance the marketing of these projects.

This chapter briefly introduces the Austrian higher education system and WU's information strategy followed by a description of three implementation projects. Implications and future developments at WU conclude this paper.

Introduction

Developing an information strategy is often done through strategic information systems planning. This refers to a process of assessing an organisational information management setting, and finding strengths and weaknesses, and based upon the results defining goals and actions for realising a strategy. Normally, planning takes place on an organisational-wide level. Consequently, an information strategy can be seen as a plan for realising goals related to hardware and software infrastructure, decision support of different groups, user satisfaction, or the creation of new services (Hansen and Riedl, 1990; Miksch, 1986).

Universities are complex organisations (Birnbaum,1989). Their services range from teaching, research, and service -- all requiring different resources and qualifications. Stakeholder universities have to serve and encompass students, parents, governments and local authorities, business, international organisations, and academic institutions. All of these groups need special attention in order to fulfil the wide social role of universities. Above all, universities' organisational structure, with its loosely coupled units working more or less independently (Clark, 1983; Cohen and March, 1974; Weick, 1976), put special burden on an effective and efficient management of academic institutions. When planning an information strategy, all these factors have to be taken into consideration (Sporn, 1992).

This chapter sets out to describe the planning and implementation process for an information strategy of one particular university in Europe: Wirtschaftsuniversität Wien (WU). The studies offered range from Business Administration (51 per cent), World Trade (33 per cent), Economics (5 per cent), Business Education (5 per cent), and PhD Studies (6 per cent). About 70 per cent of the students drop out after the first few years, and 30 per cent graduate only after 14 semesters on average.[1] Hence, WU is dealing with mass higher education, which puts a special challenge on an effective modern information strategy.

First, the Austrian higher education system and WU are described. Then, the strategic plan WU-2000 and the information strategy developed in 1994 are introduced followed by an outline of major projects implementing the new strategy. A description of planned activities and structural changes to implement the information strategy at WU conclude this article.

Austrian higher education and WU

The Austrian higher education system consists of 12 federal universities which are completely subordinate to the Ministry of Science and Research. This implies that the university budget derives almost only from the state budget and that all university staff and faculty are civil servants. Austria has no private university system. Altogether these public universities enrol about 200 000 students each academic year. After finishing high school with a diploma called the *Matura*, 31 per cent of all school graduates enter universities without paying any tuition and with a free choice of study area. Problems are high drop-out rates and the length of time to obtain a degree. Only about 10 000 Austrian students graduate each year and the average study period is around seven years, depending on the subject.

WU is one of the leading business schools in Europe. With its 20 000 students enrolled and good job opportunities, as well as an excellent reputation, the boom to study at WU does not cease, although it has been stabilising in the last years. For the winter semester 1994/95, 1 473 new students registered at WU compared with 1 460 ten years ago. WU is educating 10 per cent of all Austrian students. WU faculty is divided into 75 full or associate professors and 236 assistant professors, as well as about 300 adjunct professors. The administration consists of 240 members involved in registration, maintenance, personnel, and financial matters.

Until 1992, there was almost no management structure at Austrian universities. This changed with a reform legislation passed in 1993 (Ministry of Science and Research, 1993). Thereby, new structures and processes of universities' organisation was introduced. The underlying principle is to give more autonomy to individual institutions in order to make them more efficient and effective. Due to this precarious situation of mass education with a relatively low number of faculty and the new development of implementing management structures, the use of computers and information systems (IS) in administration, teaching, and research is crucial.

---

[1] This data is based on a collection of key data edited by the WU rector 's office dated June 1, 1994.

WU information strategy

The history of strategic planning at WU started in 1987 with the project WU-2000 (Hansen, 1987). This long range strategic plan for the university defined goals, actions, and resources for the whole institution, based upon an analysis of strengths and weaknesses of the internal structure, as well as threats and challenges of the external environment of WU. Through a wide ranging planning process that involved a large number of university members (*i.e.* faculty, administration, and students) important areas for improvement were found. The plan was then passed through all relevant WU committees for approval. This way successful implementation could be guaranteed.

One of the important areas of WU-2000 was information processing and management. The major goal in 1987 had been to establish a comprehensive, up-to-date, and quickly available choice of hardware, software, and professional end-user support. This should be achieved through stronger usage of computers in teaching and research accompanied by a trained support staff.

In 1994, a detailed plan for the information management area was released by the WU Computing Centre for the period 1994 to 1997 (Alkier and Miksch, 1994). This became necessary because of the planned reform of the university organisation, dramatically changing technology standards, and new more advanced end-user requirements. The 1994 plan was approved by the WU computing committee. It is based on WU-2000 goals as well as a survey among WU members about their technology problems and needs. Experiences of other academic institutions also became part of the plan.

To describe the problems regarding information processing at WU more specifically, the following list gives an overview of the situation in the 1990s:

- rapidly improving information technology, but a varying quality of computing infrastructure among WU departments;

- need for integration and communication between different system platforms;

- no efficient use of existing hardware and software due to lack of information,

- missing co-ordination and university-wide guidelines causing proliferation of diverse software and hardware;

- structural separation between administrative and academic computing;

- large number of inexperienced end-users needing different forms of support;

- mobile computing creating new necessary services for the users;

- stagnant number of computing personnel and budget to invest in future technology and training; and

- decrease in business contact and support caused by economic and structural problems of the information technology industry.

Based upon this situation, the goals of the organisational reform of 1993 and the WU-2000 project, the overall aim of the 1994 plan is to support WU members most effectively by providing a well organised information processing infrastructure as well as powerful IS. For the following core areas, specific objectives exist:

- *Research*: Provision of modem technology in order to reduce administrative work load for faculty.

- *Teaching:* Provision of a computing environment that enhances teaching and learning with special attention to mobile computing.

- *Administration:* Support and integration of all administrative activities in order to produce simpler, faster, and better results.

- *Top management*: Provision of a computer-based decision support system for WU top management.

These general objectives for WU research, teaching, administration, and top management have to be operationalised for the information processing area. They can be defined as follows:

- constant access to local and international information services;

- support of internal, national, and world-wide communication;

- support of all administrative work;

- use of shared databases;

- guarantee of decentralised computing for all academic and administrative staff;

- discipline and research oriented user support through well-trained staff;

- use of local and mobile computing for teaching;

- enhancement of electronic communication between students and faculty;

- faculty training in the use of information technology for teaching;

- increased use of teachware by students; and

- accounting system for computing services.

Consequently, prerequisites are necessary to enable the implementation of these goals and objectives. First, WU wide-planning and co-ordination activities have to include the network, communication, and computing infrastructure, as well as the IS development process. As a result, standards for hardware and software facilitate IS implementation, maintenance, and training. Second, all academic and administrative staff need a computer on their desks. For students, sufficient machines have to be made available throughout WU for frequent use. Third, a powerful communication platform standard is necessary for easy internal and external connections. Fourth, a data model for WU which is constantly up-dated, should serve as a basis for all IS. Finally, all this can only be achieved through professional user support.

The 1994 plan, with its goals and objectives, also defines actions for implementing the strategy. Here, a short overview is given. On one hand, these actions originate from the need to reorganise. On the other hand, more specific actions like the creation of new services and IS or a new technical infrastructure, are described. The next section discusses different projects in more detail.

Organisational consequences of the 1993 university reform also effect the information processing area. By implementing the WU reform until 1996, the administrative and academic Computing Centres form only one office called "central information services[2]". All responsibilities concerning information management of teaching, research, and administration at WU are then summarised under one umbrella. The advantage of this new structure lies mainly in the possibility to co-ordinate all development, maintenance, and training activities. At the same time, the decentralised approach prevails at WU and many users are involved in technology-related decisions.

Technical consequences that call for actions can be seen in the need for a WU-wide information management. This implies the creation of a hardware, software, and structural basis for the exchange and search of computer-based information at WU. It is extremely important that this information management can be done independently of a certain system platform, a specific site, or a special time. Through this new standard, it becomes possible to spread interesting data university-wide using an easy-to-use search tool.

Additional actions necessary for implementing the 1994 plan are constant training of computer support staff and professional marketing of services offered. Training helps that different groups, involved in computer-related work, constantly expand their knowledge about new technologies and systems. Marketing computing services through mailings, presentations, fairs, introductory courses, or press releases make the wide range of activities more visible.

The 1994 plan also needs financial resources in order to be implemented. Specific information about the budget for each project is given in the next section. At this point, general guidelines are presented. The financial situation of the information processing area as well as of the whole university is critical. A constant decrease in state budget has to be expected. This calls for cutbacks and more efficient usage of existing hardware and software. Also, the implementation of a university-wide accounting system becomes necessary. In this way, new or additional services can be charged to departments, institutes, or administrative offices.

For the development of new, or the maintenance of existing, IS at WU, university-wide standards are necessary to support easy, fast, and reliable data access. A common graphical user interface, plus a one-time log-on procedure for all IS, help to increase usage. E-mail is the base of all communication at WU. Data exchange, data search in electronic media, fax, or workgroup computing are among the features offered by electronic mail. Based on these standards, the 1994 plan defines the development of an integrated IS for top management, administration, and academic affairs.

---

[2] The German name defined by USG 93 is *Zentraler Informatikdienst.*

WU top management IS has to support all decision-making processes through up-dated and reliable data. Already existing systems, such as WUFIS for administrative work and STEP for student registration, serve as a starting point. Through new methods and techniques, quick information access and easy communication between different groups become part of the system.

The administrative IS also includes WUFIS and STEP. An additional features the participation of all relevant groups in administration. Through the 1993 organisational reform, this encompasses the secretariats of academic departments, all service offices, and some faculty. The overall goal is to make administration more transparent, faster, and easier.

The academic IS supports all students and faculty and facilitates communication between these two groups. Databases relevant for either teaching or research are made available. Through electronic mail, information between groups can be exchanged easily. Library access can also be managed through this system. Teachware, statistical packages, or math programmes are part of the offerings for academic staff and students.

This overview gives an introduction to the information strategy at WU. Many goals are listed, some actions are described, and prerequisites are outlined. What remains to be said is the implementation process of this strategy. The next section shows how WU through different, but related projects, tries to implement its information strategy step-by-step.

Implementation of WU information strategy

Despite scarce resources at WU, the quality of its technical infrastructure is above average compared with other Austrian or international universities. Only 25 staff members of the Computing Centre take care of 700 professors and administrators as well as 7 000 student users. Each year more than ATS 50 million are invested in hardware, software, and training. About 1 200 different computers (*i.e.* Apple, Digital, HP, IBM, SNI) are linked through a backbone net and connected to the Internet -- 250 of these PCs are used for student computing in labs. Central administration is supported by mainframe applications running the SNI operating system BS2000, as well as UNIX based systems. Campus licenses with software houses like Microsoft, Lotus, SPSS, or WordPerfect also enhance the development of university-wide standards.

Based on this existing infrastructure, innovative projects to implement the 1994 information strategy began. First, experiences show that financing these projects becomes possible as long as they are based on a coherent business plan. Also, computer companies are still interested in heavily supporting unconventional modem projects at universities. The marketing and public relation benefits for companies seem to over-rule economic and structural problems of the industry.

The following description of the projects PowerStore, PowerNet, and PowerPhone shows how WU uses new concepts and technology to solve its management and mass education problems. Each project is introduced showing its history, content, costs, marketing activities, and organisational consequences of the new services.

PowerStore

The first project to implement the information strategy aimed to instal a computer loan system for students using notebooks. There were several reasons for initiating this project all based on the need for wider public usage of existing computer resources in WU labs. The critical situation of seven labs with 250 computers serving about 20 000 WU students had to be mitigated by using mobile computing. Better knowledge about computer hardware and software of students and teachers made more sophisticated interdisciplinary courses in the labs necessary. Also, students increasingly wanted to work independently in the labs writing papers, theses, or searching for books and other information. An extension of space resources to create new labs was impossible. Longer lab hours were limited by legal and personnel restrictions. Above all, classes held in labs used only 50 per cent of the capacity after the first half of the semester, while others were waiting for available computers.

A solution for this precarious situation evolved when the first notebook was introduced by Apple called "PowerBook". These portable computers equiped with a built-in modem were able to solve most of the problems described above. In December 1991, a team was formed consisting of Apple and WU staff for developing an implementation concept for the new notebook loan system. The project was called "WU PowerStore" -- relating to the Apple PowerBook -- and followed these basic rules:

− PowerStore has to be self financed;

− all computers have to be delivered fully configured;

− loan and return have to be automated as much as possible;

− all computers have to be insured;

− loan prices have to be student friendly, ranging between ATS 500 to 900 per month.

In the next step, other sponsors like the Austrian Trade Commission and the Ministry of Science and Research joined the project sharing the costs of ATS 1.5 million equally. Fifty fully equipped PowerBooks were bought, and contracts for maintenance and insurance were signed. A local advertising agency was assigned the task of marketing the PowerStore project. Up until the opening of the store in March 1992, it remained uncertain as to how students, faculty, administration, and other stakeholders would react to a new service at WU which is not free of charge. It meant breaking with a long tradition at Austrian universities. In March 1992, a big event was organised and promoted for opening the PowerStore at WU. After only one hour of PowerStore existence, all PowerBooks were rented. Reservations for the next three months showed that PowerStore was a success.

After a very short evaluation period, WU decided in May 1992 to increasingly invest in the PowerStore. Since then, about ATS 8 million have been flowing out of the university budget into the project. In 1995, around 250 notebooks, most of them with a built-in modem, were constantly used. The Store not only covers its own costs but earns revenues which are reinvested. To summarise, the experiences with PowerStore demonstrate:

- that a loan system adds computing capacity, and enhances time and space-independent work;

- that services can be charged to users even in public Austrian universities;

- that a crucial success factor is professional marketing of projects; and

- that co-operation with industry is possible even during times of recession.

PowerNet

Due to communication problems at WU, a campus network system connected to the Internet available for students and staff was installed. Already at the beginning of the 1990s, WU had the most thorough local area network (LAN) of all Austrian universities. AU departments, administrative offices as well as class rooms were connected to the LAN. About 50 per cent of administrative and academic staff had e-mail accounts by 1993. Only students were not part of the network users. Consequently, improvements of teaching and administration activities could be reached by providing network accounts to the student body. An additional benefit was seen in the student experience working with new modern technology that they could use in their future job. This fast increase of the number of student users was a crucial success factor for implementing PowerNet university-wide.

As with the PowerStore, a team was formed to develop a concept following these rules:

- unlimited access for students to local network services and to the Internet;

- computer-based registration;

- user-friendly usage and error-free computing;

- high security standards;

- 24-hour free in-house access; and

- dial-in feature.

The goal to acquire 1 000 new users within the first year raised questions about financing and supporting the project through adequate numbers of staff. Several computer companies and software houses spontaneously offered their participation through money and machines adding up to ATS 1.4 million. The same advertising agency that promoted PowerStore defined a marketing strategy for PowerNet. A team consisting of members of the Computing Centre developed several applications for administering users and new on-line information services (*i.e.* course book, telephone book, electronic markets for textbooks, jobs, and apartments).

A wide-ranging media campaign for promoting the already existing WU data network ended with a big party to introduce PowerNet in the fall of 1993. The success of this event made PowerNet known nation-wide. On the day of the party, 940 new users subscribed to PowerNet. During the following weeks, a rate of 30 new users per day became standard. This huge student demand made the deletion of unused network accounts and the purchase of additional servers necessary. In 1995, six UNIX based servers and 1 200 front-end machines connected to PowerNet were installed.

This equipment serves 7 400 students and over 700 members of the faculty and administration. Services include local IS such as registration or department announcements, as well as many Internet offerings, like e-mail, netnews, gopher, or World Wide Web. Additionally, 15 computers located in one WU area called "ByteBar" provide a 24-hour access to PowerNet services. ISDN telephones enable an easy and quick remote connection to all WU services. To summarise, the experiences with PowerNet demonstrate:

– that there is a constant increase of network users after a certain number is reached;

– that administration of mass data can become totally automated; and

– that the amount of information offered by a network increases, while users become more independent of space and time, resulting in a reduction of administrative work at universities.

PowerPhone

Since 1984, WU students had been able to use a videotex system for class and exam registration as well as grade information all over Austria. In this way, administrative work was delegated to students. However, a complicated technology infrastructure, along with high costs created by an expensive price policy of federal PIT in Austria, made widespread usage and therefore the long-lasting survival of the system unlikely (Hansen, 1995). As a result, Austrian PIT wanted to move out of this market segment. Consequently, WU needed to find a technology that supported all existing functions and that could be used machine independent and nation-wide. Adoption and implementation procedures should as well be easy to manage.

The solution was found in the United States with its touch-tone based telephone systems. These systems are very useful where a high degree of standard procedures is involved. Also, they can be implemented with relatively little time and money. In spring 1994, WU examined the few available touch-tone systems in Austria. Major problems resulted from the proprietarity of the existing WU applications for student administration. It was possible though to connect one of the systems to the videotex system on the WU campus.

Since fall 1994, after some development time causing hardware and software costs of ATS 2 million, the PowerPhone and the videotex system have been working in parallel with the same database. By dialling the WU number and a specific extension, callers are connected to the PowerPhone and can then register for classes and exams as well as inquire grades information.

Due to the lack of technical resources necessary for managing a large amount of calls and queries, PowerPhone services were only offered to graduate students at first. Since the beginning of 1995, enough telephone lines have been installed to serve the entire WU student body. The only limitation is that the caller needs a digital phone. To summarise, the experiences with PowerPhone show that touch-tone based systems:

– are easy and cheap to develop;

– can be used space-independent with a standard telephone; and

– can be an alternative to regular information and ordering systems.

Implications and future developments

The implementation of WU information strategy by introducing the PowerProjects described above has major implications on the internal structure of the Computing Centre, the quality of the services offered, and the position of the computing area within WU. By integrating isolated operating units, such as user support, network services, programming, and the telephone system, processes become more efficient. Increased co-ordination between units improve the reaction time to user needs. Staff members are trained regularly and are assigned tasks according to their qualifications. Routine work becomes redundant through automation, thereby increasing motivation. Above all, technology-related issues become centrally planned and co-ordinated while leaving implementation processes to the decentralised units. By installing a user-advisory board consisting of WU students, administrators, and faculty, services offered by the "new" Computing Centre become even more user-friendly. Introducing an accounting system also enhances a "market focus" leading to the higher quality of the "products".

The development and maintenance of a coherent WU data model is the basis for all future applications. The new integrated IS especially helps to reduce the work load for all university members. The host machine is changed in order to make processes more efficient and to work machine-independent. The new system should be able to integrate WUFIS (*i.e.* WU-top management system) and STEP (*i.e.* student registration system) functions, and support the PowerPhone services. As a new project, the introduction of a machine readable chip card called "PowerCard" is planned for winter 1995. These cards store information about students or staff enabling entrance, purchase, or printing. Using this modem technology, a wide extendible range of self services can be offered to the users.

The university reform of 1993 and the information strategy of 1994 together call for a different organisational positioning of the computing area. As mentioned, the academic and administrative Computing Centre become one unit named "central information services" and support teaching, research, and administration as well as WU-top management. Agendas include planning and co-ordination, end-user support, training and marketing, as well as maintenance of WU applications and technical infrastructure. An advisory board consisting of students, faculty, and administration helps to understand user needs. It is recommended to establish a vice-rector position for information management in order to guarantee top management support. Only through an efficient structural implementation of WU information strategy can all services be offered effectively. In short, WU must increasingly invest in hardware, software, training, and marketing in order to remain among the best business schools in Europe.

REFERENCES

Alkier, L. and Miksch, G. (1994), *Zentraler Informatikdienst -- 4-Jahreskonzept der Wirtschaftsuniversität Wien 1994-1997,* Wirtschaftsuniversität Wien, Vienna.

Birnbaum, R. (1989), *How Colleges Work: the Cybernetics of Academic Organisation and Leadership,* Jossey Bass, San Francisco, London.

Clark, B.R. (1983), *The Higher Education System: Academic Organization in Cross-National Perspective,* University of California Press, Berkeley.

Cohen, M.D. and March, J.G. (1974), *Leadership and Ambiguity: The American College President,* McGraw-Hill, New York.

Hansen, H.R. (1987), *WU-2000 Entwicklungsplan der Wirtschaftsuniversität Wien 1987-2000,* Wirtschaftsuniversität Wien, Vienna.

Hansen, H.R. (1995), "A Case Study of a Mass Information System", *Information & Management,* Vol. 28, pp. 215-225.

Hansen, H.R. and Riedl, R. (1990), "Strategische langfristige Informationssystemplanung (SISP)", in Kurbel, K. and Strunz, H. (eds.), *Handbuch Wirtschaftsinformatik,* Poeschel, Stuttgart.

Miksch, G. (1986), *Strategische Informationssystemplanung dargestellt am Beispiel der Zentralen Verwaltung der Wirtschaftsuniversität Wien,* Service-Fachverlag der Wirtschaftsuniversität, Vienna.

Ministry of Science and Research (1993), *Universitäts-Organisationsgesetz* (UOG), Bundesministerium für Wissenschaft und Forschung, Vienna.

Scheuch, F. (1994), *Collection of WU Key Data,* Wirtschaftsuniversität Wien, Vienna.

Sporn, B. (1992), *University Culture and its Implications on Strategic Marketing Planning of Universities,* Physica, Heidelberg.

Sporn, B. (1993), "Analysis of the Relationship between Information Culture and Competitive Advantages in Organizations", in Eschenbach, R. (ed.), *WU Jahrestagung 1993 -- Forschung für die Wirtschaft: im Mittelpunkt der Mensch,* Service-Fachverlag der Wirtschaftsuniversität, Vienna.

Weick, K.E. (1976), "Educational Organisations as Loosely Coupled Systems", *Administrative Science Quarterly,* Vol. 21, pp.1-19.

Chapter 8

THE MANAGEMENT OF A CAMPUS NETWORK
The case of the University of Hong Kong

by

John Dockerill
City University of Hong Kong

This chapter describes the experience of the City University of Hong Kong in the management of a major campus computer network which supports around 4 000 workstations. The structure of the network is described briefly as well as the level of expenditure devoted to its support and maintenance. Management of the network has raised a number of issues particularly related to the balance between the degree of central control exercised by the university and the demand by individual departments to determine their own local network requirements.

Introduction

The City University of Hong Kong was founded in January 1984 as the City Polytechnic of Hong Kong and received its university status in January 1995. It has experienced an unprecedented growth over the past ten years, with its student population increasing by over 25 per cent for several years. It currently has a population of approximately 10 000 full-time and 7 000 part-time students studying on courses which range in level from sub-degrees to PhDs. Its discipline range includes Science and Engineering, Business Studies, Computing, Law, Social Studies and Languages.

The City University was born in temporary premises in a 20 storey office tower in Mong Kok, one of the busiest areas in Hong Kong. It moved to a purpose-built campus on the outskirts of the city in phases between 1988 and 1991. Planners for the new institution, the then City Polytechnic, realised that creating a new university-level institution from scratch offered opportunities for innovation that were rarely available to existing colleges. These opportunities included both the physical facilities to be provided and the organisational structures within which the university would operate. One of the early major planning decisions was that academic support services would be organised largely as central facilities, partly to enjoy the benefits of economies of scale and to enable such services to respond more effectively to the rapid changes in technology which were predicted to be a major feature of the 1980s and 1990s.

The development of the computing facilities was one of the major areas to benefit from this centralised approach and, as a consequence, the university has always been able to take an overall view of the needs of computers users across the institution. This enabled the growing use of networks to be exploited at a very early stage and for the necessary network structure to be incorporated into the design of the new campus.

Campus network

Figure 8.1 shows the structure of the current network. A total of around 4 000 workstations are installed on the network. Essentially the network has a two level structure. Each department has a Local Area Network driven by a server which holds a library of software items commonly used by the department concerned The server also provides some common data storage areas for the department. The second level connects all servers via main ethernet segments to a central fibre ring and hence to the central machines, information and application servers and external communication links.

The Network Software used is Pathworks 5 and the current protocol is DECNET. The network has been designed to provide all users with a physical connection to all network facilities. Software has been developed in house to provide as simple an interface as possible for the wide variety of users. This includes a menu system which simply presents a list of software packages and information services from which the user can select and choose a single password system for any service on the network.

The network is under constant development and the main central machines are being replaced. Workstations are gradually being upgraded to Pentiums and the possibility of changing from ethernet to a switching network are currently being investigated. When the campus was designed the opportunity was taken to incorporate the trunking requirements of the network into the building structure and hence changes to the network whether local to a department or affecting the major cabling runs can be easily incorporated.

Expenditure

The university has been in the fortunate position of being able to provide considerable funding for the establishment of its computing facilities. Hong Kong tertiary institutions are funded through the University Grants Committee and receives a three year block grant which is protected against salary inflation. This enables the university to plan its expenditure over the three year period with a high degree of reliability. Such a stable environment for financial planning is rarely available and has played a major role in the ability of the university to establish such enviable facilities.

Figure 8.2 shows the level of expenditure on computing over the past 7 years. The figures cover all expenditure of the Computer Services Centre. This includes staffing costs for the centre and all other expenditure, equipment, and maintenance, directly linked to the network. In recent years, the university has introduced a one-line budget for departments and there is a growing tendency for individual academic departments to purchase. Figures for recent years therefore under-estimate the overall investment of the university in computing.

The figure shows that expenditure as a per cent of the total university budget has varied between a maximum of 10 per cent to a current level of around 4.4 per cent. The peak in 1990 reflects a major investment in the network infrastructure which fortunately coincided with a major surplus on the current account for that particular year. This demonstrated one of the major advantages of the central approach to planning, enabling the university to make use of the opportunity of surplus funds to directly improve the infrastructure of its computing facilities. For comparison the university allocates around 5 per cent of its total expenditure to the library.

In terms of equipment and network cabling, it is estimated that the total investment stands currently at around US$15 million. This is actually the estimated cost of establishing the network *ab initio*. It does not include the cost of providing the physical infrastructure in the building, *i.e.* trunking. This is assumed to be zero for the City University which already has such an infrastructure in place.

Management structure

Figure 8.3 shows the structure within which the Computer Services Centre operates. The Management Board of the university is the senior executive committee of the university. It is chaired by the Vice-Chancellor and advises him on all matters relating to resource allocation, budgeting, personnel management, and the organisation and operation of all non-academic areas. The Computer Services Management Committee, chaired by a Pro-Vice-Chancellor, directly overseas the operation of the centre, including the preparation of development plans and the level of services to be provided to the university.

Figure 8.4 shows the internal organisation of the centre. This has evolved over the past ten years and reflects the changing role of the centre over this period. The network has spawned a large variety of information services, support for which has become a major role for the centre. The chart also reflects the increasing need to provide a strong systems support team for the network and the growing role of academic services. The latter provides a support service to the academic areas and concentrates on assisting the "non-computing" departments. The total staff of the centre stands at around 115 of whom some 35 are computer professionals.

Management issues

A number of management issues have arisen within the university resulting from the establishment of such a comprehensive network. Many of these are the subject of on-going debate within the institution and our experience has been that as they are resolved, or disappear, new issues arise as a result of technology advances or organisational changes to take their place.

Role of the network

One of the fundamental issues to be addressed is the role of the network in the institution. This can simply be a means of providing convenient access to computing facilities and software, and as a mechanism for informal communication throughout the institution. Alternatively the network can be viewed as an integral part of the operational and management activities of the university. City University has adopted the latter approach and sees the network as a core facility, helping the university to run the "business". This means that the network has to be professionally designed and managed. Network software has to be based on fully tried and tested products available in the market and the network has to be protected against unauthorised use which can disrupt its normal operations.

This approach can be in conflict with a minority of users, particularly computer specialists, who may wish to configure local networks for their own particular type of use and experiment with newly emerging hardware and software. This conflict is essentially an argument of centralisation or de-centralisation of facilities and has to be resolved if the network is to find general acceptance across the institution.

User philosophy

The university believes that if the network is to serve the diverse needs of the Institution, it should be designed with the non-expert user in mind. Although the need for computing support has grown from the science and engineering areas, the demands for such support has rapidly spread to all disciplines. The use of network facilities is now as great in the Humanities as in Computer Science areas. The network should be designed to provide easy access to all users even if this may appear tiresome at times to the specialist.

The university has adopted the philosophy of providing a standard user interface to the network. This was developed originally as a simple menu driven system which allowed users to select the software/service required by simply using the cursor. Associated with this has been the move towards the development of a single password system for all applications. This provides a single user/password for an individual for all services on the network, be it using e-mail, access to centrally held files, access to the personnel system, student data etc. A simple command enables a user to change their password. The university has recently moved to a Windows environment for all users. The latest phase of this is will be completed by late 1995.

Centralisation or decentralisation

This is perhaps the most difficult issue that has been faced in the management of the network and provides heated and protracted debate. Essentially those departments who have expertise in computing do not welcome conforming to the constraints imposed centrally on the network and prefer to run their own LAN based on network software of their choice.

There are, of course, Pros and Cons to centralisation. For non-expert users the central design and control of the network provides them with a secure and user friendly environment and expert support from the Computer Services Centre when required. There are clearly advantages in the central purchase of hardware, particularly if the workstations are standard configurations and central control enables the use of different software products to be monitored, simplifying considerably negotiations for site licensing. In this respect, the university has adopted a policy of acquiring as many licences as there are concurrent users of a particular product.

Communication is simplified considerably in a standard network environment, for example, if the same e-mail system is generally used across the network. The development of electronic forms and documents is facilitated in such an environment and it is easier to organise Bulletin Boards for general access and to implement network message systems both at the departmental and university level.

One of the major problems for the management of information technology is the need to constantly update users on the changes to existing products or the introduction of new facilities. Training therefore becomes a major requirement for the institution which is much easier to organise and provide when all departments operate in the same computer environment. Some standardisation of workstations on the network can reduce hardware maintenance costs considerably. This has enabled the university to establish its own maintenance team which undertakes the bulk of maintenance requirements. A conservative estimate suggests that internal maintenance costs are around 50 per cent of the current market rate.

Apart from central design and control of the network the university has also physically centralised a large proportion of the student computing facilities with around 600 workstations housed and managed by the Computer Services Centre. This has two advantages. The facilities can be managed with a minimum of staffing resources and extended opening hours can be provided to the workstation rooms. (UC Berkeley carried out a comparative study of the cost of centralising all computing facilities against complete decentralisation to the departmental level. The study showed that the latter cost twice as much as the former -- mainly as a result of staff costs.)

The main disadvantage of a completely centralised system is the constraints it can impose on specialist user departments. Centralising the development, control and operation of the network is also in conflict with the current trend for de-centralisation of other responsibilities, particularly budget control, to departments.

There is also a problem that a highly centralised system tends to suffer from a "lack of ownership". Departments do not see the facilities as part of their empire and hence have a limited commitment to their development and maintenance. Over-centralisation can also lead to network stagnation since innovation relies quite heavily on initiatives taken by the centre. It also slows down the pace of change and the speed with which new innovations can be introduced.

Some compromises

To address the major disadvantage imposed on specialist departments, the university has introduced the concept of the Autonomous Departmental Network (AND). This enables a department, if it wishes, to take full responsibility for its own Local Area Network and for the responsibility of the centre to end at the "departmental plug" which connects the AND to the main campus network. Departments are free to opt for this alternative if they feel they have the expertise to manage their own LAN and wish to be removed from the inevitable constraints imposed by a central system. Experience has shown, not surprisingly, that the main stream computing departments, together with some engineering departments, have opted for this flexibility, with all the non-specialist departments relying on the centre to install, maintain and manage their networks.

To try to avoid stagnation in the development of the network, the Computer Services Centre has established a small technology group assigned with the task of searching and examining new products as they are introduced to the market. They have also initiated several pilot projects with individual departments to test new products before implementing them more fully on the network.

The balance between the management of the facilities between the Computer Services Centre and individual departments will continue to be at the centre of debate within the institution and the exact balance will change with the introduction of new hardware and software products. However the crucial role played by the network in communication both within and outside the university requires that the development of the main network infrastructure be properly controlled and managed.

Acceptable use policies

The past few years has seen an explosion in the use of the network by students and staff for communicating with colleagues through e-mail and for obtaining access to information both locally and internationally through the Internet. To try to avoid misuse of the facility, the university has adopted an Acceptable Use Policy for the network based on similar policies adopted in North America.

The policy is published in a small pamphlet and given to all students and staff. It is unfortunate that the policy tends to be couched in negative terms covering anything that might disrupt services on the network or interfere with other users, including using their accounts for access. A copy of the Acceptable Use Policy is presented in the annex. Violation of the policy is reported to our Computer Services Centre Management Committee for action which could involve the use of the student or staff disciplinary procedures of the university. The annex also includes our "Acceptable Administrator Policy" which requires the Computer Services Centre also to accepted a set of guidelines in supporting the network.

Student access

There are issues which need to be addressed concerning student access to the network and the facilities that should be provided. These include such items as the provision and use of bulletin boards, how freely the students should have access to e-mail and the Internet. What limits should there be placed on the computer resources provided to students? How should booking systems be structured and to what extent can use of the facilities be monitored? Should the students have limited access to software, only covering items directly connected to their course of study? Is there a need to protect information available to staff or can such access be given to all members of the university including students? How does one deal with salacious material placed on the network by students?

In most of these respects, City University has adopted a very open approach to these matters and provides students with the maximum access and facilities. There is a growing need to support off-campus access to the network for students. City University does not have student residences but, where they are provided the student rooms should be wired into the network. This is the case at the university of Science and Technology in Hong Kong and is being adopted as a standard requirement for the development of new residences. For students studying from home, access needs to be provided through a dial-up service. Most students now have their own PC at home and the dial-up service is becoming a major feature of the computing service provided by the university.

One of the major problems in providing so many workstations throughout the campus is the amount of space that has to be provided. To provide a reasonable environment for the students, it is estimated that approximately $3m^2$ (net) is required. Space in Hong Kong is a particularly scarce resource and, at market rates, $3m^2$ (net) represents an annual cost to the university of around US$1 500, which is more than the average cost of most of the workstations. Portable computers are therefore a very attractive alternative for providing general access to the network. To explore their use, the university has installed a number of "plug in" points to the network where students and staff can connect and use a portable machine.

Administrative data-processing

The university has a range of administrative data processing systems which have been implemented over the past ten years. These include student, financial and personnel systems and inventory systems for space and other assets. In addition the library has cataloguing and circulation systems developed internally including both English and Chinese titles. The university also implemented an Executive Information System some three years ago which is built on the operational DP systems and extracts information to an EIS Database. EIS is currently available on some 100 workstations. The introduction of new applications to EIS is the responsibility of the Management Information Office of the university.

Distributed access to desegregated data, centrally held, is a more recent development and several systems are now available for on-line access to all departments. The use of electronic forms is growing with a number of examples already implemented including a new purchase and requisitioning system.

The university is actively pursuing the application of Business Process Re-engineeing (BPR) and currently has three re-engineering projects underway. It recognises that this will have a major impact on its requirement for IT support and that its new systems must move to a client/server basis to support the re-engineered processes.

Future developments

Technology

Planning for the future in a rapidly developing environment is a particularly difficult task. However there are clear trends in the use of the network which point to immediate tasks for the university. Use of the network for both internal and external communications grows at an alarming rate and the speed and capacity of the current installation is unable to cope with the increasing demand. One of the immediate tasks therefore is to upgrade its speed and capacity. This problem is exacerbated by the development of multi-media applications. The university installed a separate video distribution system in its early years based on a simple point to point manual switching system which enabled video material to be distributed to all lecture theatres and classrooms. This system is about to be replaced by a video on demand system which will use the computer network as the vehicle for distribution. This will again increase the demand for speed and capacity on the network.

The problem and cost of accommodating such a large number of workstations on campus will increase the move towards the use of portable machines and the provision of plug-in sockets to the network. The university is considering schemes to provide a loan pool of portables for student use and the possibility of helping students to purchase their own portable machines.

Management

It is envisaged that the trend for departments to operate their own Local Area Networks will continue and the number of Autonomous Departmental Networks will increase. The role of the Computer Services Centre will shift to concentrating on the basic infrastructure of the main network and the development of central information services for the university. It is also anticipated that the training role of the centre will grow substantially together with the provision of effective help and trouble shooting services.

CPNET acceptable user policy

1.1   Users should not interfere with the work of other users on the network or disrupt network services, and should not deliberately attempt to degrade the performance of host systems or any devices on the network.

1.2   Electronic communications facilities (such as E-mail and Bulletin Board) should be used for non-commercial activities only. Any communication which violates the Laws of Hong Kong or is undesirable for the City University of Hong Kong is not to be sent or stored.

1.3   Loopholes in network security systems, or knowledge of special passwords etc., should not be used to disrupt the network services or to use any resources on the network for which proper authorisation has not been given.

1.4   Users shall not intentionally interfere with, or alter, the integrity of the network. Such actions include unauthorised use of accounts, impersonation of other individuals in communications, attempts to capture or break passwords, attempts to break encryption protocols, compromising privacy, destruction or alteration of data or programs belonging to other users, etc.

1.5   Users shall not intentionally or knowingly create or distribute "worms" or virus programs on the network, and shall take all reasonable precautions to prevent such actions.

1.6   Computer software protected by copyright may not be copied from or onto the network, except as permitted by law or by the contract with the owner of the copyright. (*e.g.* users are not permitted to copy PC software from the various software libraries onto their personal storage devices.)

1.7   A user accounts assigned to an individual by the Computer Centre or a department, may not be used by others without explicit permission from the assignee. The individual is responsible for the proper use of the account, including proper password protection.

1.8   Users should not attempt to connect or disconnect equipment of any sort (*e.g.* computers, bridges, routers, repeaters, protocol analysers, data loggers, cables, transceivers, BANC connectors, etc.) to/from the network which may degrade the integrity of the network without first seeking permission from Computer Services Centre. Computer Services Centre shall not prevent such connections/disconnections unreasonably and shall provide full justification for such action.

1.9   It is unacceptable to conduct experiments on the network that demonstrate network vulnerabilities without the prior permission of the Computer Services Centre.

1.10   Users should apply network address from Computer Services Centre for their networked workstations to avoid conflicts which might result in disruption of normal operation of the network.

1.11   All users should comply with the acceptable CREN Use Policy, Bitnet Usage Guidelines and Internet Acceptable Use Policy (RFC 1087).

1.12   Autonomous sub-net managers and users shall comply with this policy insofar as it applies to their operations.

CPNET acceptable administrator policy

2.1   Computer Services Centre will not normally make changes to the network or its functionality without full and timely consultation with faculties/college. Nor will it normally make such changes during a semester or summer term without prior approval of faculties/college. Timely consultation means *e.g.* providing sufficient time for departments/divisions : to budget for and acquire necessary hardware and/or software to support the changes to the network, to develop and implement revised teaching/learning instruments, etc. Where an urgent requirement causes Computer Services Centre to make changes without prior consultation, Computer Services Centre shall make every effort to communicate its actions as soon as possible to the affected users.

2.2   In order to maintain the integrity of the network, Computer Services Centre reserves the right to allow or disallow the use of any computer software on the network. Computer Services Centre shall not exercise this right unreasonably and shall provide full written justification for such action.

2.3   Network addresses of all network nodes should be centrally assigned by Computer Services Centre to avoid conflicts which might result in disruption of the normal operation of the network. Likewise, assignment of network node names should be co-ordinated by Computer Services Centre.

2.4   To protect the integrity of the network and to protect authorised users from the effects of unauthorised or improper use, Computer Services Centre reserves the right to limit or restrict any account holder's usage, inspect, copy, remove or otherwise alter any data, file, or system resources which may be causing the disruption. Computer Services Centre shall not take such action unreasonably and shall provide full written justification for such action.

2.5   Computer Services Centre shall take all reasonable actions to protect against loss of data in its efforts to maintain the integrity, privacy and security of the network facilities but disclaims responsibility for loss or for its necessary interference with files.

Figure 8.1 **Structure of the campus network**

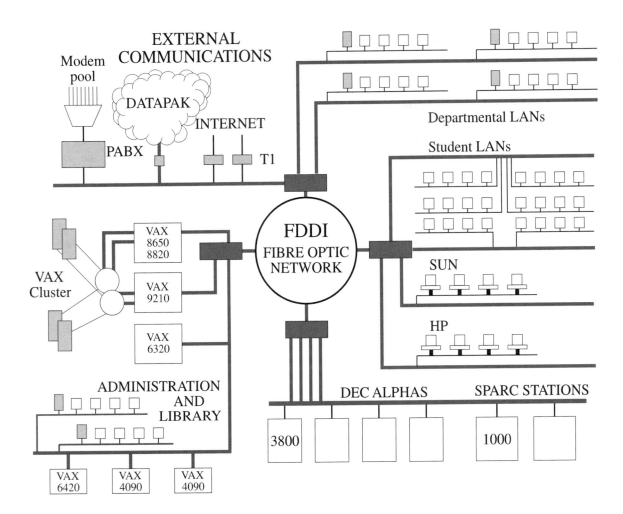

Figure 8.2 **Level of expenditure on computing**

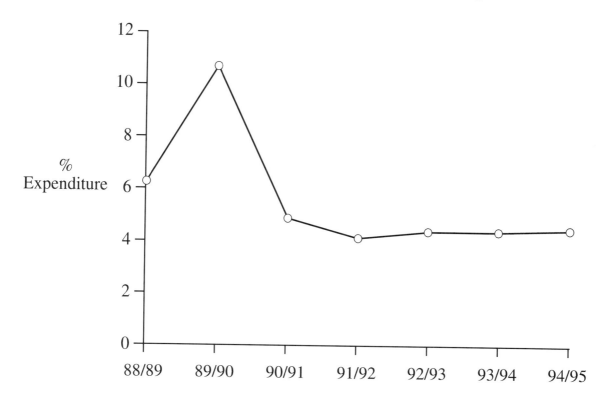

Figure 8.3 **Management structure**

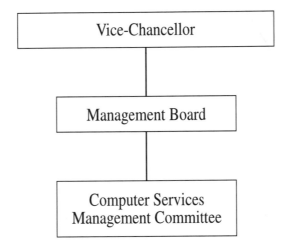

Figure 8.4 **Internal structure**

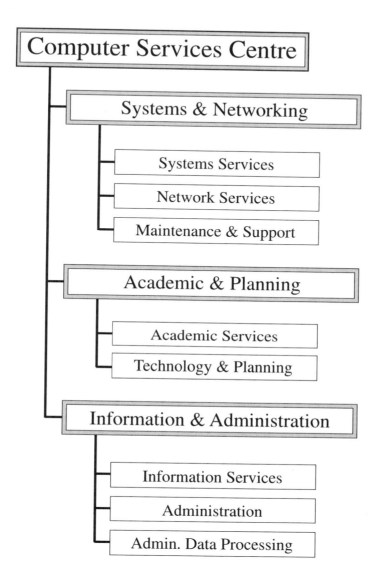

Chapter 9

INFORMATION STRATEGIES
A UK Perspective

by

Peter Ford
University of Nottingham, United Kingdom

Introduction

It is now fashionable for universities to develop (and even be required to develop) information strategies along with other strategic issues concerned with Estates management or "teaching and learning". In a recent survey of UK universities regarding their progress in implementing information strategies, one institution produced the following response:

"We do not have an information policy as such, nor do we have a satisfactory definition of what an information policy is. There is a lot of talk about institutional information policies but no-one has yet nailed their colours to the mast and defined what it encompasses and, more importantly, what it will achieve."

This level of candour was not widespread among the respondents, many of whom claimed to have developed an appropriate strategy, either in whole or in part. However, the bulk of the responses gave clear indications that there is great confusion between an *Information Technology* strategy and an over-arching *Information* strategy, with the former often driving the latter.

The case for an information strategy

At the basic level of an information technology or systems strategy it can be argued that they are merely an articulation of how technology can assist "that which is already done", to be done better. Such strategy documents are valuable in themselves, since they are likely to define standards and introduce coherence into an often chaotic situation. However, they do not critically address the fundamental questions such as: what information does an institution actually need; how does it create or acquire it; and to whom, and how, should it be disseminated. As such, they are little more than fashion accessories -- nice to have, but providing little added -- value in themselves. If, however, it is accepted that a university must have well-defined business processes in order to service its objectives, a case for business process re-engineering becomes apparent. Taking a fresh look at information needs thus offers a more radical, and potentially more rewarding, step which can streamline current practices; eliminate others; and embrace new approaches as technology and costs allow.

A typical research-based university in the United Kingdom now has an annual turnover well in excess of £100 m, with the largest ones approaching £200 m. By any standards these are significant multi-faceted businesses in their own right. These universities are now facing very real challenges in the coming years, of which the following are some of the most pressing:

- a major increase in student numbers;
- a steady decline in the unit of resource;
- spiralling costs of books/periodicals;
- raised expectations from students for self-paced learning;
- modularisation of degree courses;
- quality issues for teaching and research;
- changes in student age profiles;
- competition across the higher education sector; and
- the need to manage ancillary businesses to maximum efficiency, e.g.
  - catering and residential services,
  - security services,
  - conferences,
  - estate management,
  - power management.

In order to address many of the above issues there is a need for substantive investment. Yet many institutions are barely in a financial "break-even" situation and have relatively modest cash reserves. Thus, to generate the necessary cash for investment this scenario needs to be turned into one of generating sufficient surplus of income over expenditure to enable adequate resources to be ploughed back into the business. In the light of this and given that the very core of a university is based on the creation and dissemination of information, it seems reasonable to conduct a major review of information needs and information flow covering all aspects of teaching and learning, research, provision of scholarly information and the administration of the ancillary businesses, in order to maximise the opportunities for future investment.

The current scene

As with any organisation, the starting point for the information strategy should be the strategic objectives of the university and its plans for achieving them. The planning steps needed to put this into effect are already well defined. However, whilst the necessary steps are usually well known, it is clear that few institutions have sought to pursue them in a systematic way.

In the United Kingdom, the Higher Education Funding Councils (HEFCs) now require all universities and HE colleges to prepare institutional strategies. These are intended to start from the mission, objectives and onward developing plans. In theory, at least, all institutions have therefore defined their broad objectives. Unfortunately some of these are so broad that they give no meaningful guidance as to the direction of the institution. Thus "to be at the leading edge of teaching and learning" is not particularly useful for planning purposes. Some institutions have, however, taken this process much further, but relatively few have analysed their activities, costed and prioritised them and developed plans reflecting these priorities and the likely resource implications.

Such approaches have, on occasions, been applied to the administrative activities of the institution rather than the academic ones -- despite the former's greater cost and importance. Defining *information* in the broad sense, it is essential to start with a clear sense of direction for the whole of the institution -- and particularly for the academic side. Without such an analysis and its resulting

sense of direction, it is difficult, if not impossible, for a university to develop an overall information strategy. However there are some who question the extent to which a university can have concise "strategic objectives" at the level of the institution as a whole. With a few exceptions, most institutions are so diverse -- and so driven by to the varying demands of students, employers, accrediting bodies and the Funding Councils -- that it may be that little meaningful can be said about them at the institutional level. A university which only has meaningful strategic objectives for its academic purpose at the school or department level may find it difficult to have meaningful institution-wide strategies for anything else.

A UK information initiative

To encourage institutions to confront these issues, the Joint Information Systems Committee of the four UK Funding Councils produced in 1995, with the help of Coopers and Lybrand, an Information *Framework Document*. This identifies the key issues which might be required to draw up an information strategy; thus providing the means whereby a particular institution can take from the framework those ingredients applicable to their specific mission and objectives and to then create an information strategy which meets their specific needs. From this high level strategy then flows a number of lower level planning documents, namely :

- an academic information systems strategy; defining information provision for the academic processes (with major involvement from the library);

- a management information systems strategy to support the required business processes; and

- an underpinning information technology strategy defining the infrastructure and standards which apply to it.

What differentiates universities?

The nature of higher education institutions varies widely -- although of course some are more different than others. There are many reasons for these differences, some historical, some intentional and some accidental. In terms of developing an information strategy at least two major questions need consideration:

- What parameters define the essential differences between institutions?
- Which of these generate the need for a different elements of a framework for the development of an information strategy?

Important differentiators might include:

- the size of the institution;
- student mix (e.g. proportion of part time students, mature students, overseas students);
- the balance between teaching and research;
- the nature of research undertaken (e.g. "blue sky" or "applied");
- the subject range of undergraduate teaching;
- the existence of a medical school;
- the extent and nature of links with outside organisations (e.g. funding sources, accreditation bodies);

- the methods adopted for learning (e.g. use of Computer-Assisted-Learning, open/distance learning);
- site configuration (i.e. multiple campuses);
- decision-making structures (e.g. use of committees, devolved budgeting); and
- current information provision and systems.

The success of the information strategy depends on identifying those factors which *really* matter from the point of view of producing a framework. This does not equate with identifying those factors which matter when producing an information strategy. For that, all the factors will matter, albeit to varying degrees. Thus, those factors which really matter will critically depend on what is envisaged by a *framework*.

The decision-making processes

Any framework is useful only in so far as there are mechanisms within an institution to use it to develop a tailored information strategy. Again this is much easier in the administrative area since, in most institutions, there is usually a clearly identified person who has the responsibility to develop administrative computing systems which meet the institution's requirements. It is still unusual for an institution to have designated an individual, or even a committee, with responsibility for overall information needs. Indeed the very nature of information makes it most unlikely that individual academics would be content for their use of information systems to be subject to control by such a body.

Whilst this does not mean that the resulting framework will not be used, it does mean that the chances of it being used in a coherent way are reduced unless positive steps are taken to make this happen. For example, it is now recognised in some organisations outside higher education that information is as important a resource as others on which the organisation depends (e.g. finance); thus responsibility for it is placed at board level. Some institutions also recognise this, with responsibility being held at Pro-Vice-Chancellor level. This works well when the individual concerned is knowledgeable about information in their own right, but this is relatively rare. Where such arrangements do not exist (and that is in most institutions), the people responsible for the various components of information are often of more junior status than their academic colleagues --thus making it even more difficult to pull together all the threads of an information strategy.

Of course none of this makes the development of a framework impossible within an institution, just more difficult. It is important to recognise this point and to include a development of it within the framework.

The nature of a framework

The framework must:

- be relevant and applicable to the HE environment and adequately reflect the diverse needs of the sector;

- be practical in terms of what institutions can reasonably be expected to achieve within the resources likely to be available to them; and

150

– demonstrate that there are real benefits to institutions from having such an information strategy (from improved quality and/or reduced costs) which outweigh the investment required.

These criteria must be used to test the validity and value of the framework which is produced.

It is recognised that the need for an institution-wide framework should not necessarily lead to an institution-wide system. More generally, there is perhaps a tendency for organisation-wide information strategies to lead to attempts to centralise computing power and authority. An open mind must be kept on this both from the point of view of academic pragmatism but also to ensure that, where they apply, the real benefits of distributed computing over a major central system can be recognised.

Ingredients needed to develop a framework

In order to build a framework from which strategic plans can be developed an institution needs to carefully examine the following issues:

Vision

- What is the mission?
- What is the business strategy for:
  - teaching and learning,
  - research,
  - resource management?
- What plans exist for IS/IT?

Information needs

- Who needs information?
  - students, academics, administrators
- What information is needed?
- Where are the sources of information?
- Who are the recipients?

Information management

- What is the information flow throughout the institution?
- How is information gathered, stored and disseminated?
- Do individuals co-operate over information flow?
- How is IT used?
- Is there an identifiable budget for information flow?
- How effective are these activities in contributing towards the objectives of the institution?

Negative factors

- Are there problems in the following areas?:
  - definition of information needs, standards, relevance, ownership, accuracy, timeliness, completeness, consistency, status, presentation;
  - security;
  - procedures;
  - awareness;
  - use and supply;
  - external liaison;
  - audits; and
  - roles and responsibilities.

- Can the costs associated with these be identified?

Example of activities and outputs

To illustrate the processes which are necessary to create the elements of a framework, it will be necessary to break down the "top level" objectives into their component parts to establish the appropriate information flows. As an example, consider the mission "to effectively manage teaching and learning". This might be analysed as overleaf (see Figure 9.1).

Development of the framework

Resulting from the analysis above, the framework should be used to piece together the appropriate strategy. In this context, current thoughts are that a framework might include, for each element:

- Applications:
  - the systems that should be developed/enhanced;
  - the information needed;
  - who should use them?;
  - how should they be developed?;
- Technology infrastructure:
  - definition of the technology/processors/databases;
  - definition of the networks;
  - definition of the standards to be used;
- Organisation and management structure:
  - the balance of centre/local/outsourced resource;
  - the training strategy;
  - the information management strategy;
- Business case:
  - what cost for what benefit?;
- Transition plan:
  how do we get there from where we are?

Figure 9.1

Level 1	Level 2	Level 3	Level 4
To effectively manage teaching and learning	Develop teaching/ learning strategy	Know institutional vision for types of teaching learning Know institutional resource capacity for teaching/learning Know market demand Know external requirements Know competition in teaching/learning (and collaboration arrangements) Develop plans for teaching activities	
	Deliver effective teaching/learning	Design course/module and assessment	Agree curriculum/ assessment methods Investigate and agree delivery mechanisms Review resource requirements Review previous performance Confirm student demand Obtain validation and approval of course
		Prepare/assemble resources	Develop (or obtain) course/module materials Timetable course/module delivery Ensure provision of consumables Ensure provision of non-consumables Ensure appropriate space (including for disabled)
		Deliver and assess courses/modules	Communicate course delivery arrangements Deliver courses/modules Assess student performance
		Conduct performance review	Collect performance information Evaluate performance Assess quality of teaching and staff performance Deliver training programme for staff

The objective in determining a framework for how institutions should develop their own information strategies will be to maximise the benefit to them of adopting an appropriate and consistent strategy which allows lessons to be learned without suppressing creativity. Many initiatives which have attempted to create a solution providing the greatest good for the greatest number have collapsed under their own weight. In developing the framework for action it is important that such mistakes are not repeated. The framework needs to be based on what is practical, feasible and acceptable. Also identified, and included within the framework, must be the management actions which have to be undertaken to enable the initiative to be successful.

Implementation

Creating and implementing an information strategy for higher education institutions is a difficult and complex process. It requires both thought and action. The following points articulated by Professor Enid Mumford might usefully be borne in mind.

Strategy is an emergent process

Examining the present and creating the vision of the future is the start of the strategic planning process but is by no means the end. Strategy, in practice, tends to be an emergent process rather than a rational one. Small steps are taken which provide information and a new basis for action and this process continues until the desired change has been accomplished.

The strategy must be flexible

Because the university environment is constantly changing, the strategy must also change and be flexible. A strategy developed at one particular time and implemented at another is almost certainly flawed as circumstances will have altered. Tightly structured visions, developed at one moment in time, are useful academic exercises but can prove to be a liability if they are implemented without establishing that they still fit new circumstances and needs.

The strategy must fit the culture

Terms such as "competitive edge", "business process re-engineering", "total quality", "value chains" are becoming commonplace. Many of these are old ideas given new names and associated with a great deal of marketing hype. Many of these initiatives fail unless they fit closely with a particular culture and are introduced with great care. Instead of improving efficiency, the result can be a major increase in costs, staff hostility and a set of new and unfamiliar problems.

Risk analysis and evaluation should be continuous

Risk analysis and evaluation should be ongoing and continuous. Many risks can be avoided if they are anticipated and evaluation should form part of the learning process.

Conclusions

It is too early to predict a successful outcome to this *framework* approach. However, early signs are encouraging in that institutions have already volunteered to become pilot sites in trialling implementation. The need for a "top-down" information strategy is rapidly gaining acceptance in the more progressive institutions who see it as an important tool in reducing overheads and facing the challenges of the next decade. It is expected that some six pilot institutions will be selected, representing a range of traditional and newer institutions -- both large and small. Each will be provided with assistance from a centrally funded co-ordinator who will feed back to a central steering committee the experiences, both good and bad, with a view to refining the framework document and widely disseminating best practice. Once these exemplars are available, it is confidently expected that tangible and measurable cost benefits will become visible to, and accepted by, the whole community.

MAIN SALES OUTLETS OF OECD PUBLICATIONS
PRINCIPAUX POINTS DE VENTE DES PUBLICATIONS DE L'OCDE

AUSTRALIA – AUSTRALIE
D.A. Information Services
648 Whitehorse Road, P.O.B 163
Mitcham, Victoria 3132   Tel. (03) 9210.7777
                              Fax: (03) 9210.7788

AUSTRIA – AUTRICHE
Gerold & Co.
Graben 31
Wien I   Tel. (0222) 533.50.14
                              Fax: (0222) 512.47.31.29

BELGIUM – BELGIQUE
Jean De Lannoy
Avenue du Roi, Koningslaan 202
B-1060 Bruxelles   Tel. (02) 538.51.69/538.08.41
                              Fax: (02) 538.08.41

CANADA
Renouf Publishing Company Ltd.
1294 Algoma Road
Ottawa, ON K1B 3W8   Tel. (613) 741.4333
                              Fax: (613) 741.5439
Stores:
61 Sparks Street
Ottawa, ON K1P 5R1   Tel. (613) 238.8985
12 Adelaide Street West
Toronto, ON M5H 1L6   Tel. (416) 363.3171
                              Fax: (416)363.59.63

Les Éditions La Liberté Inc.
3020 Chemin Sainte-Foy
Sainte-Foy, PQ G1X 3V6   Tel. (418) 658.3763
                              Fax: (418) 658.3763

Federal Publications Inc.
165 University Avenue, Suite 701
Toronto, ON M5H 3B8   Tel. (416) 860.1611
                              Fax: (416) 860.1608

Les Publications Fédérales
1185 Université
Montréal, QC H3B 3A7   Tel. (514) 954.1633
                              Fax: (514) 954.1635

CHINA – CHINE
China National Publications Import
Export Corporation (CNPIEC)
16 Gongti E. Road, Chaoyang District
P.O. Box 88 or 50
Beijing 100704 PR   Tel. (01) 506.6688
                              Fax: (01) 506.3101

CHINESE TAIPEI – TAIPEI CHINOIS
Good Faith Worldwide Int'l. Co. Ltd.
9th Floor, No. 118, Sec. 2
Chung Hsiao E. Road
Taipei   Tel. (02) 391.7396/391.7397
                              Fax: (02) 394.9176

DENMARK – DANEMARK
Munksgaard Book and Subscription Service
35, Nørre Søgade, P.O. Box 2148
DK-1016 København K   Tel. (33) 12.85.70
                              Fax: (33) 12.93.87

J. H. Schultz Information A/S,
Herstedvang 12,
DK – 2620 Albertslung   Tel. 43 63 23 00
                              Fax: 43 63 19 69

Internet: s-info@inet.uni-c.dk

EGYPT – ÉGYPTE
Middle East Observer
41 Sherif Street
Cairo   Tel. 392.6919
                              Fax: 360-6804

FINLAND – FINLANDE
Akateeminen Kirjakauppa
Keskuskatu 1, P.O. Box 128
00100 Helsinki
Subscription Services/Agence d'abonnements :
P.O. Box 23
00371 Helsinki   Tel. (358 0) 121 4416
                              Fax: (358 0) 121.4450

FRANCE
OECD/OCDE
Mail Orders/Commandes par correspondance :
2, rue André-Pascal
75775 Paris Cedex 16   Tel. (33-1) 45.24.82.00
                              Fax: (33-1) 49.10.42.76
                              Telex: 640048 OCDE
Internet: Compte.PUBSINQ@oecd.org

Orders via Minitel, France only/
Commandes par Minitel, France exclusivement :
36 15 OCDE

OECD Bookshop/Librairie de l'OCDE :
33, rue Octave-Feuillet
75016 Paris   Tél. (33-1) 45.24.81.81
                                   (33-1) 45.24.81.67

Dawson
B.P. 40
91121 Palaiseau Cedex   Tel. 69.10.47.00
                              Fax: 64.54.83.26

Documentation Française
29, quai Voltaire
75007 Paris   Tel. 40.15.70.00

Economica
49, rue Héricart
75015 Paris   Tel. 45.75.05.67
                              Fax: 40.58.15.70

Gibert Jeune (Droit-Économie)
6, place Saint-Michel
75006 Paris   Tel. 43.25.91.19

Librairie du Commerce International
10, avenue d'Iéna
75016 Paris   Tel. 40.73.34.60

Librairie Dunod
Université Paris-Dauphine
Place du Maréchal-de-Lattre-de-Tassigny
75016 Paris   Tel. 44.05.40.13

Librairie Lavoisier
11, rue Lavoisier
75008 Paris   Tel. 42.65.39.95

Librairie des Sciences Politiques
30, rue Saint-Guillaume
75007 Paris   Tel. 45.48.36.02

P.U.F.
49, boulevard Saint-Michel
75005 Paris   Tel. 43.25.83.40

Librairie de l'Université
12a, rue Nazareth
13100 Aix-en-Provence   Tel. (16) 42.26.18.08

Documentation Française
165, rue Garibaldi
69003 Lyon   Tel. (16) 78.63.32.23

Librairie Decitre
29, place Bellecour
69002 Lyon   Tel. (16) 72.40.54.54

Librairie Sauramps
Le Triangle
34967 Montpellier Cedex 2   Tel. (16) 67.58.85.15
                              Fax: (16) 67.58.27.36

A la Sorbonne Actual
23, rue de l'Hôtel-des-Postes
06000 Nice   Tel. (16) 93.13.77.75
                              Fax: (16) 93.80.75.69

GERMANY – ALLEMAGNE
OECD Bonn Centre
August-Bebel-Allee 6
D-53175 Bonn   Tel. (0228) 959.120
                              Fax: (0228) 959.12.17

GREECE – GRÈCE
Librairie Kauffmann
Stadiou 28
10564 Athens   Tel. (01) 32.55.321
                              Fax: (01) 32.30.320

HONG-KONG
Swindon Book Co. Ltd.
Astoria Bldg. 3F
34 Ashley Road, Tsimshatsui
Kowloon, Hong Kong   Tel. 2376.2062
                              Fax: 2376.0685

HUNGARY – HONGRIE
Euro Info Service
Margitsziget, Európa Ház
1138 Budapest   Tel. (1) 111.62.16
                              Fax: (1) 111.60.61

ICELAND – ISLANDE
Mál Mog Menning
Laugavegi 18, Pósthólf 392
121 Reykjavik   Tel. (1) 552.4240
                              Fax: (1) 562.3523

INDIA – INDE
Oxford Book and Stationery Co.
Scindia House
New Delhi 110001   Tel. (11) 331.5896/5308
                              Fax: (11) 332.5993
17 Park Street
Calcutta 700016   Tel. 240832

INDONESIA – INDONÉSIE
Pdii-Lipi
P.O. Box 4298
Jakarta 12042   Tel. (21) 573.34.67
                              Fax: (21) 573.34.67

IRELAND – IRLANDE
Government Supplies Agency
Publications Section
4/5 Harcourt Road
Dublin 2   Tel. 661.31.11
                              Fax: 475.27.60

ISRAEL – ISRAËL
Praedicta
5 Shatner Street
P.O. Box 34030
Jerusalem 91430   Tel. (2) 52.84.90/1/2
                              Fax: (2) 52.84.93

R.O.Y. International
P.O. Box 13056
Tel Aviv 61130   Tel. (3) 546 1423
                              Fax: (3) 546 1442

Palestinian Authority/Middle East:
INDEX Information Services
P.O.B. 19502
Jerusalem   Tel. (2) 27.12.19
                              Fax: (2) 27.16.34

ITALY – ITALIE
Libreria Commissionaria Sansoni
Via Duca di Calabria 1/1
50125 Firenze   Tel. (055) 64.54.15
                              Fax: (055) 64.12.57
Via Bartolini 29
20155 Milano   Tel. (02) 36.50.83

Editrice e Libreria Herder
Piazza Montecitorio 120
00186 Roma   Tel. 679.46.28
                              Fax: 678.47.51

Libreria Hoepli
Via Hoepli 5
20121 Milano   Tel. (02) 86.54.46
                            Fax: (02) 805.28.86

Libreria Scientifica
Dott. Lucio de Biasio 'Aeiou'
Via Coronelli, 6
20146 Milano   Tel. (02) 48.95.45.52
                            Fax: (02) 48.95.45.48

JAPAN – JAPON
OECD Tokyo Centre
Landic Akasaka Building
2-3-4 Akasaka, Minato-ku
Tokyo 107   Tel. (81.3) 3586.2016
                            Fax: (81.3) 3584.7929

KOREA – CORÉE
Kyobo Book Centre Co. Ltd.
P.O. Box 1658, Kwang Hwa Moon
Seoul   Tel. 730.78.91
                            Fax: 735.00.30

MALAYSIA – MALAISIE
University of Malaya Bookshop
University of Malaya
P.O. Box 1127, Jalan Pantai Baru
59700 Kuala Lumpur
Malaysia   Tel. 756.5000/756.5425
                            Fax: 756.3246

MEXICO – MEXIQUE
OECD Mexico Centre
Edificio INFOTEC
Av. San Fernando no. 37
Col. Toriello Guerra
Tlalpan C.P. 14050
Mexico D.F.   Tel. (525) 665 47 99
                            Fax: (525) 606 13 07

Revistas y Periodicos Internacionales S.A. de C.V.
Florencia 57 - 1004
Mexico, D.F. 06600   Tel. 207.81.00
                            Fax: 208.39.79

NETHERLANDS – PAYS-BAS
SDU Uitgeverij Plantijnstraat
Externe Fondsen
Postbus 20014
2500 EA's-Gravenhage   Tel. (070) 37.89.880
Voor bestellingen: Fax: (070) 34.75.778

NEW ZEALAND –
NOUVELLE-ZÉLANDE
GPLegislation Services
P.O. Box 12418
Thorndon, Wellington   Tel. (04) 496.5655
                            Fax: (04) 496.5698

NORWAY – NORVÈGE
NIC INFO A/S
Bertrand Narvesens vei 2
P.O. Box 6512 Etterstad
0606 Oslo 6   Tel. (022) 57.33.00
                            Fax: (022) 68.19.01

PAKISTAN
Mirza Book Agency
65 Shahrah Quaid-E-Azam
Lahore 54000   Tel. (42) 735.36.01
                            Fax: (42) 576.37.14

PHILIPPINE – PHILIPPINES
International Booksource Center Inc.
Rm 179/920 Cityland 10 Condo Tower 2
HV dela Costa Ext cor Valero St.
Makati Metro Manila   Tel. (632) 817 9676
                            Fax: (632) 817 1741

POLAND – POLOGNE
Ars Polona
00-950 Warszawa
Krakowskie Przedmieácie 7   Tel. (22) 264760
                            Fax: (22) 268673

PORTUGAL
Livraria Portugal
Rua do Carmo 70-74
Apart. 2681
1200 Lisboa   Tel. (01) 347.49.82/5
                            Fax: (01) 347.02.64

SINGAPORE – SINGAPOUR
Gower Asia Pacific Pte Ltd.
Golden Wheel Building
41, Kallang Pudding Road, No. 04-03
Singapore 1334   Tel. 741.5166
                            Fax: 742.9356

SPAIN – ESPAGNE
Mundi-Prensa Libros S.A.
Castelló 37, Apartado 1223
Madrid 28001   Tel. (91) 431.33.99
                            Fax: (91) 575.39.98

Mundi-Prensa Barcelona
Consell de Cent No. 391
08009 – Barcelona   Tel. (93) 488.34.92
                            Fax: (93) 487.76.59

Llibreria de la Generalitat
Palau Moja
Rambla dels Estudis, 118
08002 – Barcelona
                   (Subscripcions) Tel. (93) 318.80.12
                   (Publicacions) Tel. (93) 302.67.23
                            Fax: (93) 412.18.54

SRI LANKA
Centre for Policy Research
c/o Colombo Agencies Ltd.
No. 300-304, Galle Road
Colombo 3   Tel. (1) 574240, 573551-2
                            Fax: (1) 575394, 510711

SWEDEN – SUÈDE
CE Fritzes AB
S–106 47 Stockholm   Tel. (08) 690.90.90
                            Fax: (08) 20.50.21

Subscription Agency/Agence d'abonnements :
Wennergren-Williams Info AB
P.O. Box 1305
171 25 Solna   Tel. (08) 705.97.50
                            Fax: (08) 27.00.71

SWITZERLAND – SUISSE
Maditec S.A. (Books and Periodicals - Livres
et périodiques)
Chemin des Palettes 4
Case postale 266
1020 Renens VD 1   Tel. (021) 635.08.65
                            Fax: (021) 635.07.80

Librairie Payot S.A.
4, place Pépinet
CP 3212
1002 Lausanne   Tel. (021) 320.25.11
                            Fax: (021) 320.25.14

Librairie Unilivres
6, rue de Candolle
1205 Genève   Tel. (022) 320.26.23
                            Fax: (022) 329.73.18

Subscription Agency/Agence d'abonnements :
Dynapresse Marketing S.A.
38, avenue Vibert
1227 Carouge   Tel. (022) 308.07.89
                            Fax: (022) 308.07.99

See also – Voir aussi :
OECD Bonn Centre
August-Bebel-Allee 6
D-53175 Bonn (Germany)   Tel. (0228) 959.120
                            Fax: (0228) 959.12.17

THAILAND – THAÏLANDE
Suksit Siam Co. Ltd.
113, 115 Fuang Nakhon Rd.
Opp. Wat Rajbopith
Bangkok 10200   Tel. (662) 225.9531/2
                            Fax: (662) 222.5188

TRINIDAD & TOBAGO
SSL Systematics Studies Limited
9 Watts Street
Curepe
Trinadad & Tobago, W.I.   Tel. (1809) 645.3475
                            Fax: (1809) 662.5654

TUNISIA – TUNISIE
Grande Librairie Spécialisée
Fendri Ali
Avenue Haffouz Imm El-Intilaka
Bloc B 1 Sfax 3000   Tel. (216-4) 296 855
                            Fax: (216-4) 298.270

TURKEY – TURQUIE
Kültür Yayinlari Is-Türk Ltd. Sti.
Atatürk Bulvari No. 191/Kat 13
Kavaklidere/Ankara
                            Tel. (312) 428.11.40 Ext. 2458
                            Fax: (312) 417 24 90
Dolmabahce Cad. No. 29
Besiktas/Istanbul   Tel. (212) 260 7188

UNITED KINGDOM – ROYAUME-UNI
HMSO
Gen. enquiries   Tel. (0171) 873 0011
Postal orders only:
P.O. Box 276, London SW8 5DT
Personal Callers HMSO Bookshop
49 High Holborn, London WC1V 6HB
                            Fax: (0171) 873 8463
Branches at: Belfast, Birmingham, Bristol,
Edinburgh, Manchester

UNITED STATES – ÉTATS-UNIS
OECD Washington Center
2001 L Street N.W., Suite 650
Washington, D.C. 20036-4922 Tel. (202) 785.6323
                            Fax: (202) 785.0350
Internet: washcont@oecd.org

Subscriptions to OECD periodicals may also be
placed through main subscription agencies.

Les abonnements aux publications périodiques de
l'OCDE peuvent être souscrits auprès des
principales agences d'abonnement.

Orders and inquiries from countries where Distribu-
tors have not yet been appointed should be sent to:
OECD Publications, 2, rue André-Pascal, 75775
Paris Cedex 16, France.

Les commandes provenant de pays où l'OCDE n'a
pas encore désigné de distributeur peuvent être
adressées aux Éditions de l'OCDE, 2, rue André-
Pascal, 75775 Paris Cedex 16, France.

                                           5-1996

OECD PUBLICATIONS, 2, rue André-Pascal, 75775 PARIS CEDEX 16
PRINTED IN FRANCE
(91 96 08 1) ISBN 92-64-15309-8 – No. 49039 1996